[soft] magazine is a quarterly magazine that publishes conversations and interviews between young artists/creative people. Each issue, we will publish 6–8 artist interviews, as well as introduce works from an emerging young artist.

aaajiao, 29 years old, Shanghai

Interviewed in *K11*, Shanghai
September 15th, 2013

Can you introduce yourself, what do you do?

I have been working in the field of New Media Art for almost 10 years now. I've also co-founded a co-working space in Shanghai, called *Xin Danwei*. Nowadays, I work a lot with commercial organizations, or cooperate with them as an art consultant.

Wait, so what exactly do you do? Are you an artist or an art event curator?

Well, in the past year or two, many commercial spaces in China such as shopping malls or real estate projects have felt the need to become 'artsy'. It's a trend that's coming in a very direct way. They may choose to do contemporary art, or new media art. So what we do is to help them build an overall art structure, advise them how to let their project make sense in an artistic context, as well as for the general public.

Is it difficult to find a good balance between art and commerce?

In fact, from my experience, it's never a problem in terms of curating content. Because the content of art is rather simple, once you find the right thread, you can start to make simple resources plentiful. I think it's a bit abstract to talk about this. But in general, no, it's not a difficult thing. The difficult part is how do you win their trust, not of how to get the actual work done.

For example, the *K11* project you are currently working on, can you talk about it more specifically?

We started the *K11 project* at the beginning of 2013. Our main job is to help them organize all the cultural events, such as lectures, creative workshops, etc. What we do is quite different from the public educational events the museums have to offer. We make it more of a variety, and we focus on presenting artists themselves. We do a lot of artist talks. And we do artist talks as their own events, instead of in conjunction with the exhibition.

Artists have the chance to present their work and way of thinking to the audience, and that's what makes audiences interested. What audiences are not interested in are the theoretical academic discussions of art, because that's something they cannot understand. So that's one basic difference we have with museums.

We also recommended curators to *K11* to curate open exhibitions for their soft opening and grand opening exhibitions. And we curated a series of events according to these exhibitions.

What changes do you see happening in the art circle in Shanghai in recent years? It seems to me there is more and more cooperation between art and fashion happening these days.

Let's put it this way, there was always cooperation between art and fashion, that's a fact that has never changed. Perhaps now, the younger generation we are familiar with is starting to have a very quick connection with the fashion world. The older generation probably was doing the same thing before, but we were not in their context, so we didn't know about it. And you don't pay attention to this kind of stuff solely. But I think the cooperation between art and commerce, especially with real estate, or with offline spaces has increased quite obviously. It's not the same as the gallery mode, the for-profit or nonprofit art space modes, but in the form of direct real estate art or the shopping mall mode. It has a very clear business model, and has been recognized by the public, the same as the gallery mode, the for-profit or nonprofit art space modes, but in the form of direct real estate art, or the shopping mall mode. It has a very clear business model, and has been recognized by the public.

Let's talk about your own creative works.

Well, I've had two solo exhibitions in the last

two years. They were shown in art spaces and galleries. At the end of this year, there will be another solo show but presented at two different locations at the same time. One will be in a traditional art gallery space, the other will probably be in *K11*, because I have a good relationship with them and they want to support young artists too. So, from my point of view, my pace hasn't changed much, I've always been making things at this pace.

Is there any difference to you between having an exhibition in a gallery vs at shopping mall?

I think there are differences. I mean I will take the target audience into consideration. When I show my work in a shopping mall, I will think about the decorative factor of the work within the space, or how my work is going to be broadcast. I will take those elements into consideration. When showing in a gallery, I would adopt the simple artist's mindset, maybe I will consider the fact that galleries want to sell work. But it depends on the artist. To me, my works are not easy to sell at galleries, so I basically don't think about whether it's going to sell. Once the gallery agrees with my proposal, then I will carry it out my way. I won't change my project for them. But when exhibiting in public space like shopping malls, I will think about the audience, maybe design the work to be more interactive.

What is your average day like? How much time do you spend on your own creation, and how much on other commercial projects?

Actually, in the past couple years, most of my time is spent on meetings, having meetings with all different kinds of people. I also write a lot of emails. Most of the things are not relevant to my own creation. But I'm also used to living like this. I won't say I need to find a specific time to make the work, or say I need to sit in my studio and spend time thinking about the work. This won't happen to me. Most of my ideas come from little threads of daily life, I keep the habit of searching for these little threads. Gradually, these threads will form a concept for the bigger work. It's a daily process, and it's hard to say how much time I've spent on it. I can say I'm spending time on my ideas everyday, or I can say I don't have a fixed time to do this. Most of my time is spent on communicating with different kinds of people and resources these years. Mostly I'm dealing with problems related to business matters.

Do you have to find the balance between your personal life and your creative life? Or is it not a problem for you?

I think I will keep on making commercial installations and multimedia business projects, since I've been doing it for quite a few years. But I've been doing these types of projects with a team, so it's a studio project, it does not really have much connection with my personal life. Maybe it's a case of that, I bring back the project, and they realize it. So I won't think it's taking up too much of my personal life. Because it's a system that's already built, so there's inertia.

What about the financial part? Can you make enough money to support yourself?

So far so good. I've done a lot of business where I've lost money. But there is always a way to balance it.

I think the old mentality is that artists have to hold on when they are poor.

I think it depends on your age. If we were discussing this 3–5 years ago, I may say 'Yes, you have to hold on.' And I think now, a lot of young artists are still hanging in there. But when you grow older, your skills will get better. And when your skills get better, you should be able to solve your living problems. If you can't solve it, then I'm afraid it's a matter of abilities.

As far as you know, what's the situation like with other artists living in Shanghai?

In general, there is a lack of energy. I don't know if it's because they have too much living pressure, or it's just their way of looking at things. I think there is a lack of energy for young people. A lot of the time they are making very standard art works, but you always feel like there is something missing, something lively or ingenious. They are making a work, but not a work that can touch you. Very few works will give you intuitive feelings. Of course you can say there are many reasons for this phenomenon. Many people say this generation is like this, they are very self-centered, that's why. But in my opinion, when I'm looking at a work, I'll looking at if the work is like its creator. This is my very direct sense. I think it's a matter of sincerity. This genuineness will come through the technique, the process of expression. These will all be reflected through the work. That's my standard for recognition of work, at least it's a genuine expression. Even if the work sucks and the artist sucks, at least I think he's very direct.

But what I see in most of the young artists in Shanghai is that their work might look very good, but you are not convinced that it's done by them, or you don't see the connection between the artist and the work. So it's really hard to say if this is right, or what should be right. There are both sides of the coin. But for me personally, I'd still prefer genuine works. To me, if you can already decorate your work very well by technique when you are young, I don't know how you go further and make progress in your work. Because this type of work, it can look like anyone else's work. Then you lose the uniqueness about it.

How do you see the difference between artists in Beijing and artists in Shanghai?

I'm less and less familiar with Beijing nowadays. Every time I go to Beijing, or if there are friends coming from Beijing, I always ask them about what's going on there now. But it's hard to tell, in my impression there is not much change compared to the structure before. You can still tell quite clearly which artist is from Beijing, and which one is from Shanghai. You can tell by the work.

I've heard that there are more resources over there, and it might be better to move there, career-wise.

Look at the facts. Let's just look at the year 2013. There are actually more opportunities in Shanghai than in Beijing. Many artists are considering moving here actually. Because in Shanghai, it's easier to get things done. We used to say, Beijingers like to 'talk too much, but do nothing.' Which means, artists think a lot, but they never make the work. Maybe years ago, many people like this kind of idea, but in recent years, many young artist are growing, and their thoughts are changing. They might start to like a place where there are clear rules. Also, in Shanghai there are so many commercial opportunities. Or, let's say it's a place that makes you feel grounded. I think many artists need this. So, Beijing and Shanghai are still two totally opposite places. But regarding opportunities, I don't think Shanghai has less than Beijing. They are more or less the same.

How do you look at the problem of living in big cities, where your living cost is very high while at the same time there are

so many things happening every day, so much information. As an artist, you have to find your way, time and status to create. Is this a problem for you?

To me, I think if you are taking it as a problem, then it's a problem for all people who are living in big cities. But I'm not taking it as a problem. I think of course there will be problems, everyone has his or her problems. You can't escape such social structure and pace of life. It annoys me, but it's not a problem.

What's your plan for the following year?

I don't really have a plan. These past two years, most of the time when going abroad, I'm going as a tourist. Not like before, where it was mostly because of festival invitations. I think this has to do with the general environment of economic crisis. I didn't have to pay anything when I went to

Europe years ago. But last year when going to America, I had to spend my own money. So it has to do with the logic of foundations, or their interest in China. But I'm not really planning to go abroad or anywhere. I'm still following my own logic.

In your experience, do you find any difference between foreign artists and Chinese artists?

From the context that I'm most familiar with, media art, I see artists are doing very similar things. This is a very obvious point in comparison with contemporary art. We are all making work under the same concept. The way you get your information, what you are concerned about, it's all very similar, because media art is rooted in the background of globalization, or different kinds of details happening under the environment of online culture. Maybe the form of expression, or the debate on certain topics is different, but the essential part is still quite similar. So I was always saying, it's a fair game for video art. If you are making good works, it's going to be good for all over the world. But if it's bad work, it's not going to work anywhere.

Last question, can you talk about your thoughts on the current status of Chinese society other than art? Politics, economy, etc…

I think it's like the boiling frog experiment. As the frog, you don't have a very clear sense of what's going on, but there might be a critical point. Either you decide you are going to stay here for the rest of your life, or you choose to start a new life somewhere else.

Do you want to leave?

I should have been applying for OPE immigration to the US. But I find it's too complicated, and I don't have time to do this kind of thing at the current pace of my life.

But you know once you move over there, you are going to lose all the resources here?

Yeah, it's a reality. And a problem I'm not in a hurry to deal with.

aaajiao (aka *Xu Wen Kai*) currently works as an emerging new media artist. His works are represented by *Leo Xu gallery* in Shanghai. He has run 10 kilometers every day for the past 3 years.

www.eventstructure.com

aaajiao，29岁，现居上海

2013年9月15日
采访于上海K11购物艺术中心

自我介绍一下你是做什么的？

我是主要做新媒体艺术，做了差不多快十年。但我同时做过一个co-working space在上海，叫新单位。然后我现在也在跟很多商业机构，或者说一些机构合作，帮他们做艺术顾问。

你到底是怎样的一个身份？是艺术家还是艺术活动策划？

其实就是说，可能这一两年在中国很多商业的空间，就是完全商业的，像商场。或者说它是一个地产类的项目，它对艺术类的需求越来越高了。比前两年要高很多。而且属于这种……它也很直接，它可能就是会选择做当代艺术，或者做新媒体艺术。那我们其实就是说去帮它做一个整体的艺术构架。告诉它如何在艺术的线索里成立。然后也告诉它如何在公众的面前成立。

你觉得这难做吗？能不能找到好的平衡点？还是会太商业？

其实从我的经验来说，我们从来就觉得从内容的规划上不是个难事儿。因为其实艺术的内容比较单一。就是说你只要找对线索，你就能把这些单一的资源做地比较丰富。我觉得这个比较抽象。但是，总地来说，不是一个难的事儿。难的是你怎么取得他的信任。而不是说难的是做这些事情。

比如说你现在在做的K11的项目？你能具体谈一下吗？

K11购物中心其实是从13年年初就开始做的。我们做的主要的工作就是帮助他们做所有的活动。这些活动包括做讲座，做创意，做workshop。然后这些活动我们就区别于美术馆的公共教育活动。我们做得比较多样化。而且我们更多地是突出艺术家本身。我们做过很多艺术家讲座。这个讲座并不是挂着展览来做的，而是单纯地做艺术家讲座。

艺术家把他做的作品和他的思维方式呈现给大家。然后这个时候其实很多观众对这个是感兴趣的。而观众不感兴趣的是那种基于艺术或基于某种艺术线索的具体讨论，其实观众是听不懂的。而且他也没什么太大的兴趣。这个是我们一个方向性上的区别。另外一个就是我们也推荐了策展人给K11为它做soft opening和grand opening的开幕展览。然后我们也根据这些展览做一系列活动。

这几年上海的艺术圈和艺术生态有什么变化？我这次回来好像看到有很多艺术和fashion的紧密合作。

我觉得这么来说吧。其实和fashion的合作从来没变过，一直就有。只是可能到现在，我们所接触的年轻的群体开始跟时尚有了一个比较快的接触。可能以前老一辈的艺术家在做。你不在它的线索里，所以我们不知道有这样的事儿。你也不会去单独关注这样的事。但我觉得商业跟艺术的结合，尤其是地产类的，在线下有空间类的跟艺术的结合是明显地多的。不是以前的画廊模式或者说这种盈利或者非盈利的艺术空间的模式。而是直接的地产艺术的形式。或者是shopping mall的形式。它是有很明确的商业模型在的。而且被大家认定是可以成立的。

能不能再讲一下关于你自己的创作的部分？

我其实这两年做过两个个展。都是在艺术空间或者画廊做的。然后今年年底会再做一个个展但是在两个地方发生。一个还是在传统的画廊艺术空间。另外一个可能就会选在K11，因为跟他们有一个比较好的关系，而且他们也希望支持年轻艺术家来完成一些东西。所以这个，从我的角度来讲，我的步伐基本是没有特别大变化，还是以这个节奏在做东西。

对你自己来说，你在画廊做和在shopping mall做展览有什么区别吗？

我觉得还是有的。就是我们还是会考虑受众的问题。我们在商场一定会考虑受众。它的整个逻辑的装饰性，或者说它的这种被传播的能力。我们就会把它考虑在展览的因素里。而在画廊做可能更多的还是很简单的艺术家思路。可能会兼顾一点点画廊的这种买卖的要求。但是这个分艺术家的。从我的角度来讲，我的作品因为不是画廊一般能卖掉的。所以我其实不考虑画廊能不能卖的问题。他只要同意做，我就按照我的方法来做，不改方案的。但是反而在这种比较广义的公共空间里做会考虑受众。需要有一些在设计或者说在环节上的设置让大家更有参与性。

你每天的日常生活安排是怎样的？有多少时间你可以用来做自己的创作，然后又有多少时间是用在做其他的商业计划？

其实这一两年我做的最多的事情就是开会。跟各类人开会，然后回邮件。很多跟自己的创作关联不大。然后也是我的习惯，就是说我不会特意找一段时间说，哦，我最近要做作品了，我要坐在工作室，或者坐在一个地方去想作品。这个对我来说不大成立。我的很多东西都是其实我一直会有一个习惯，就是去搜集一些小的零碎的线索。这些线索慢慢最终变成了作品的概念，融到我的大的作品的概念里。我觉得这个是很日常的。我很难说是花了多长时间。我可以说是每天都做，我也可以说没有一个固定的时间来做。但是其实花时间的更多是这几年在跟各类人，各类资源在沟通。然后很多是很事务型的问题。

对你来说，你需不需要去找个人生活和作品创作之间的平衡点？

我觉得因为我做商业的装置或者多媒体的商业项目做了很多年了，所以我还会继做。但是这个因为我有 t e a m ，所以更多是变成了工作室的项目，跟我其实私人的关联并不大。可能是我拿回来的一个项目最终变成他们来实现，这样子。所以我不会特别觉得占用很多时间，因为那个更像一个惯性的东西。

那经济方面呢，够养活自己吗？

暂时看起来还好。而且还做过很多亏本的生意。那么这个是有方法来平衡的。

好像过去通常的思维会是，如果要做艺术家就得死扛着。

我是觉得这个可能也分年纪吧。你如果说三，五年前你跟我讨论这个问题，我可能会说，真的，是会是扛着。我觉得现在很多年轻的艺术家也是在扛着。但是随着年龄的增长，你的很多技能会比之前要更熟练，或者说是更有技巧性。所以你在增长这些技能的同时，你其实也应该要能把你的生活问题解决掉。如果解决不掉，我觉得我只能说可能是能力问题。

就你所了解到的上海其他的艺术家，他们是怎样一个生存状态？

嗯，总的来说我觉得缺乏一定的活力。我不知道是说他们的生活压力，还是他们本身看待事情的看法。我觉得就是缺少一种年轻人应有的活力。我觉得他们很多时候在做很标准的艺术，但是你会觉得缺乏那种生动的部分，或者说巧妙的部分。他们做的是一件作品，但是，就很少能感动你，或者说，很少的作品会有一个比较直观的感触。我觉得这个有很多种讲法，很多种层次。很多人讲说，这是这一代人的东西，就是这样的，因为都是相对比较自我。它就会形成这样一种格局。但是我会觉得，我有时候在看，就是说有很多作品不像他的人。这是我很直观的一个感受。所以我觉得这个里面就有真诚的问题，就有在使用技法上的问题。表达的这种过程中的问题。我觉得都会出现在他们身上。我会比较认可一种方式，就是说他的作品就和他的人很相似。我觉得这是一个很真诚的表达。可以是很烂的作品，他也可以是很烂的人。但我觉得起码他很直接地去做这样一件事儿。但我看到更多的上海的年轻艺术家，他们的作品可能做得非常好，但是你觉得不像是他们能做出来的。或者说跟他联系不大。所以你很难讲，是不是对，或者说可能这个才是对。这种就会有两面性。但是从我个人的喜好来说，我还是更喜欢更直接一点的东西。我觉得在年轻的时候，如果你已经可以用很高的技巧去修饰作品的话，我不知道他怎么再往前进一步。因为到之后修饰出来的东西，他可以像任何人的东西，我觉得就会失掉这种特性。

你怎么看北京和上海的艺术家的区别？

其实北京我现在越来越不了解。我每次去北京，或者说每次有北京来的朋友我都会问。讲不大清楚，但是我觉得可能跟之前的格局没有特别大的变化。你还是可以很清晰地分出，哪个艺术家来自北京，哪个艺术家来自上海。从作品还能看出来。

我听说那边可能资源比较多，去那边可能有更好的发展？

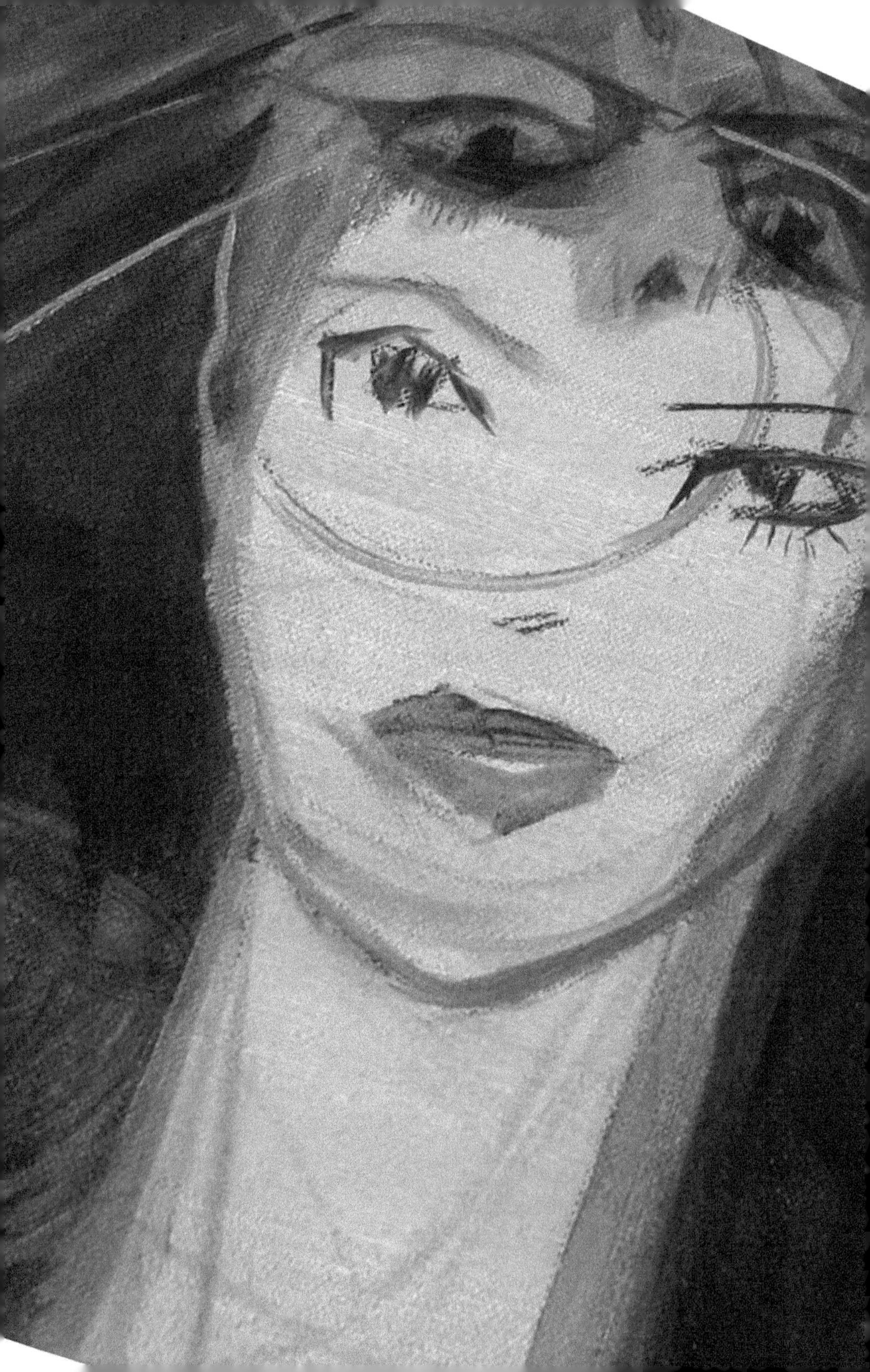

其实从现实讲，13年这一年，上海的机会比北京多得多。而且很多艺术家也在考虑来上海。因为上海可能变得更容易有一个能落实的东西。我们其实

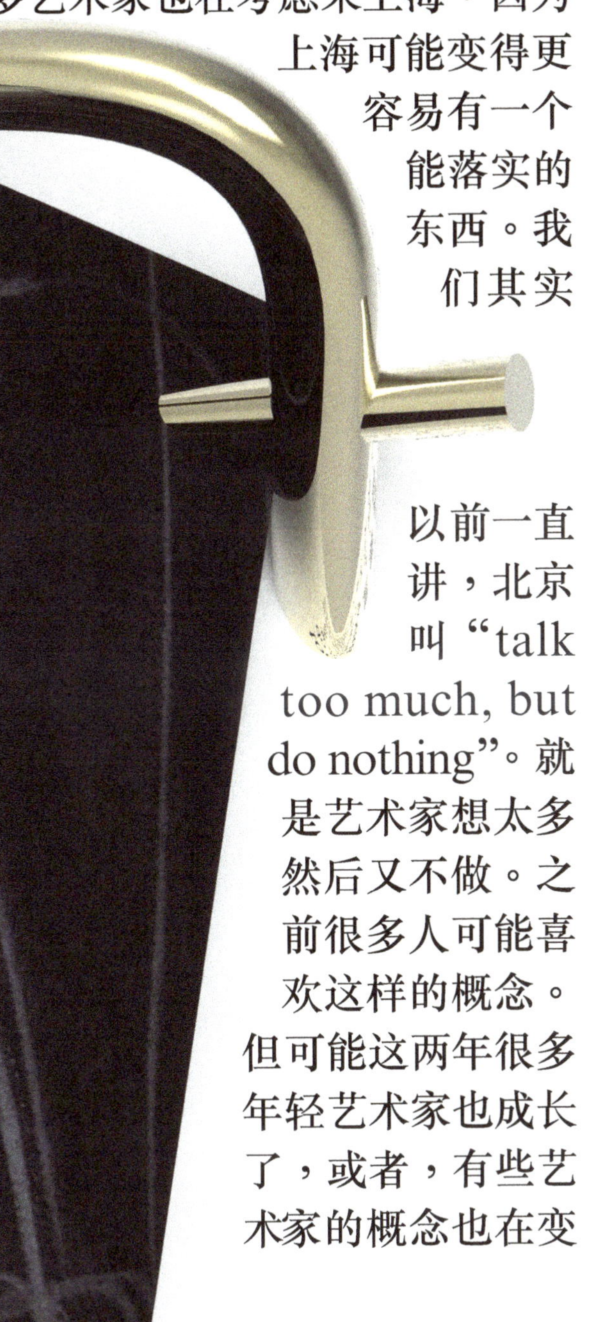

以前一直讲，北京叫“talk too much, but do nothing”。就是艺术家想太多然后又不做。之前很多人可能喜欢这样的概念。但可能这两年很多年轻艺术家也成长了，或者，有些艺术家的概念也在变

化。他可能更喜欢一个有明细规则的地方。然后这儿可能有好多商业的机会。或者说这儿有一种更好地能让你踏实下来的感觉，我觉得很多艺术家也需要。所以北京上海还是两个极端。但是在机会上，我现在没有觉得北京比上海要多多少，其实差不多。

你怎么看，生活在大城市，生活成本这么高，一方面，有太多的信息，太多的事情在发生。然后作为艺术家又要能够找到创作的时间和状态。对你来说，这是不是一个问题？

对我来说，如果你把这个归纳为困扰的话，我觉得这是生活在大城市所有人的困扰。但是如果把它当作问题来说，我没有把这件事儿给变成一个问题。我觉得困扰是有的，我觉得每个人都会有这样的困扰。这是你逃不掉的一个社会结构跟一种生活的节奏。但是它不是我的问题。它是我的困扰。

接下来几年你有什么样的打算？

接下来倒没有。其实这一两年，到国外去更多的就是去看一看嘛。还不像以前很多是艺术节的邀请。我觉得这个跟整个的大经济环境有关。以前去欧洲我从来没有掏过一分钱，但是我去年年底去美国的时候就是我自己来掏钱。所以就说跟整个foundation的逻辑，或者说对中国的关注有关。但是我没有特别打算要去国外或者去哪。我觉得还是按照我自己的逻辑在慢慢走。

就你所接触到的国外的艺术家，你觉得和国内的艺术家的状态有什么区别吗？

其实我觉得从我最熟悉的语境，从这种媒体艺术的语境，其实大家做的事儿及其相似。这个比当代艺术要明显。就是说大家真的是在同一个概念下在做事情。因为你所有获取信息的方法，你关注的点，都是极像的。原因是这件事根植于一个所谓的“全球化”，或者说一个大的互联网环境下和语境下发生的各种小细节。极其像。只是说可能表现形式，或者是某种辩题上有很明显的区别，但是本质是极像的。所以我一直也在讲说，我觉得video art这事儿，从来就很公平。你做的好，你在全世界就会都做得好。你做得不好，你在任何地方都不成。

最后一个问题，你能不能谈一下，除艺术以外，你生活在中国现在的社会状况里面，政治，经济环境啊各方面，你有没有一些什么想法？

其实我觉得这就像温水煮青蛙。你作为那只青蛙其实你没有很明显的感触。但是可能有临界点。临界点就是要不然你就彻底在这儿就呆了。要不然你就选择，想办法换一个地方生活。

你想离开吗？

我其实应该申请ＯＰＥ做人才移民去美国。但我嫌麻烦，就是在我现在的生活节奏里面，应该做不了这事儿。

但是你过去之后就没有这边这么多资源了？

对。所以这个是现实。也是一个不急于去处理它的问题。

aaajiao（徐文恺）目前以新媒体艺术家的身份工作并且为人所熟知。他的作品被上海的Leo Xu画廊代理。**aaajiao**每天坚持跑步10公里已经3年。

www.eventstructure.com

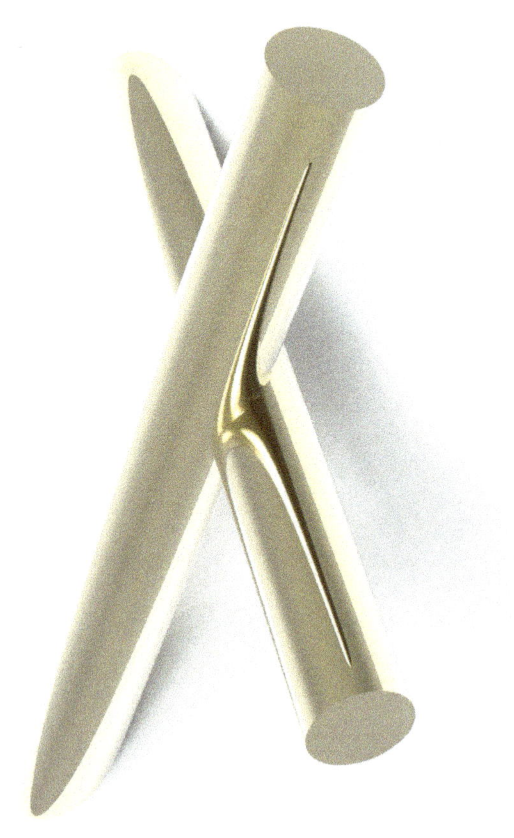

Cara, 26 years old, Shanghai (from Belgium)

Interviewed at Donghu Rd, Shanghai.
January 3rd, 2015

Please introduce yourself.

Hi, my name is *Cara Toes*. I'm originally from Belgium. I live in Hong Kong now. And I'm a street artist, muralist. I prefer muralist actually. Yeah, some people say it sounds really old school, but I think it's a nicer word.

What about graffiti artist?

No, no. I'm definitely not a graffiti artist. What I discovered is that people who are street artists don't like to be called graffiti artists, and graffiti artists don't want to associate with street art.

How are they different?

Well, graffiti is more letters and bombing. And street art is not letters. There are a lot of rules in the graffiti world. But because I started doing murals totally on my own, I don't have the background of those histories and stuff, so I don't know. I mean, I just want to paint. I just want to paint walls.

How do you like Shanghai?

I really like it. It's pretty crazy, cause it's so random. But I like Shanghai. I think Shanghai is a really cool city. It's so different from Hong Kong. People here are so international, and I like that even though you guys are international, you guys can merge with the local people in a really good way. While in Hong Kong, it's very separate.

Did you have an art or painting background from college?

No, I studied biochemistry at the University of Genk. And then after that, I studied game design. But I was horrible at it. I studied that because I wanted to learn the craft.

So you just started painting all by yourself?

Well, I've been drawing forever, but I thought that was normal. When I was 22 or 23, I realized not everyone could draw. When I was younger I was always shy about my drawing because I thought it was shit. I guess I still have that now. So I started doing street art a little bit in Amsterdam, but I had a full time job, so... but in Hong Kong I was living in such a tiny space, I went totally crazy. So I went to the streets, and started painting walls every night everywhere on my own. And I felt like I accomplished something.

So how does it work for you job-wise? Do you just do mural painting for fun? Or can you make a living out of this?

So I painted in the streets of Hong Kong. And then, suddenly this guy said, 'Oh, you paint? Let's paint together.' And then, I snuck into a big group show in Hong Kong. It was one of the biggest ones yet, because street art painting was new in Hong Kong.

So there were a lot of big names, and there was a gallery involved and everything. And I painted a really big wall there. And the gallery saw it, and they offered me a solo show, together with a commissioned wall for a restaurant. It was crazy, 'cause I spent my last money for the ticket to go to the place, 'cause it was not near where I live. And I spent 2 days working on it nonstop. And then, they gave me the money, and with that money I could do my solo show.

And then, from then on, a lot of things started happening. Like now, I live on my own. I also did murals for the Facebook office in Hong Kong. And then, after that, I was like, oh shit, what now? You know, so I did a lot of murals and live events. And then, after I finished the Facebook mural, I kind of felt like, I don't know what to do now.

Why? Is it because Facebook was a big milestone for you?

I wouldn't call it a milestone, ok, yeah, maybe. But it was more like ah shit… like at first, it was like, every week I was really scared. Like, shit man, about future jobs, about how am I going to do lalala… but things just kept on going. And I was really busy all the time. And Facebook happened. And I didn't know what my goal was. So, after that, I was like empty. I got some jobs, but I wasn't really happy with it, 'cause I felt like it was really becoming a job, instead of something that I would put my heart into it.

So then, I went on a trip on my own to America for a month and a half, and ever since, I have been travelling nonstop. 'Cause I found out I really enjoyed it. And when I travel abroad, I can actually get jobs. And with that money, I can travel somewhere else, so I've been doing this for just over half a year.

Are you happy with your life right now?

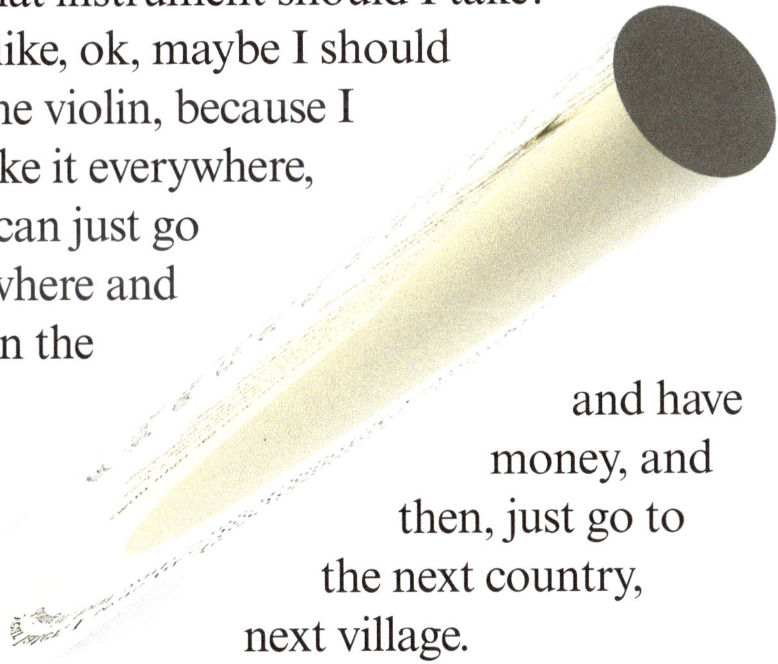

I'm absolutely really intensely happy, cause everything is all what I wanted. Like when I was a kid. I think I was 7 or 8, I would lie in my bed, and think, ok, what do I want? I said, hmm, I would really like to travel, everywhere. At that point, I also played music, and when you are 7 or 8, you need to pick your first instrument. I was like, ah, what instrument should I take? I was like, ok, maybe I should take the violin, because I can take it everywhere, and I can just go somewhere and play on the street and have money, and then, just go to the next country, next village. And then, now, so many year later, I was like, fuck man, I was really doing it, but with something way better. This is way better, cause it goes together with the whole society. Like the whole street art scene, like all these people are so nice. They do it for the passion, for the fun. So, the people who are doing it, we already all have the same kind of mindset. We don't think about the money, no one thinks that I will just do it for the money. I think a lot of other jobs you just do it for the money. But this is just like, we can paint together, and some people we don't even speak the same language, but we paint, and you can tell that's a universal language.

Is street art still illegal in most places? Do you have to hide or paint at night?

Yeah, well, that's the thing. Of course it's illegal. They have terms like 'bombing', where you go at night and you write your name. That's more like graffiti. But the thing is, like now it's more accepted. If I see a wall, and I think the wall is really nice, I will just ask the owner if I can paint it. So then, it doesn't have to be illegal, so I can make something beautiful, and spend some time on it. Cause in the end, all I wanted to do is to make something that will change the environment and people will come by.

What is this desire to paint on a wall outside on the street rather than just paint on a canvas in the studio?

It reaches so many more people. When I was in Amsterdam, I was biking to work, and sometimes I would see some graffiti, and I would be like 'that's not nice.' And also, I will be thinking in my situation, what would I want to see if I bike to my work, you know? It's fun to see something surprising, and the environment change. Like one day, you see this cat eating a cookie, or this other thing.

When I was living in Amsterdam, I started thinking about everything I wanted to do when I was a kid. And I think it's very important to realize that you can change. You can just do whatever you want. Cause I think, you know, from my Asian background, it's always like you can never do what you want. Always do what your parents say. Always think before every decision you make, 'ok, what would my parents say if I do that?' I don't want to embarrass them. I was raised very strictly.

But in Amsterdam, because it was a different country, I started thinking about what do I want. You know, I never really thought about what I really want. I'd been almost doing everything just so maybe my parents could be proud of me. Just say 'Hey, nice job!'

Do they know what you are doing now? Do they appreciate that?

Now, finally. The thing is I think they never worried about my work life or my studies, cause I always do very well. Before, when I was studying biochemistry, they had no clue what it was. And when I was doing game design, they didn't know either, they never played games.

With murals, it's something so simple. I just paint on the wall, I would show them a picture, in a restaurant, people sitting there, and they understand what it is. 'Cause it's so basic. That's the beauty of doing murals. It's universal. And also like because I moved to Hong Kong, people would write articles about me, or something like that. It's in Chinese, so they can read it. So they can finally understand.

And definitely the Facebook thing, my parents came to visit me. And we were sitting in this restaurant, and suddenly it showed on the national television on the wall. And my parents… just by chance, you know, I don't have a television, and they barely watch it. But we were in a restaurant, and they showed it on television. And then I knew ok,

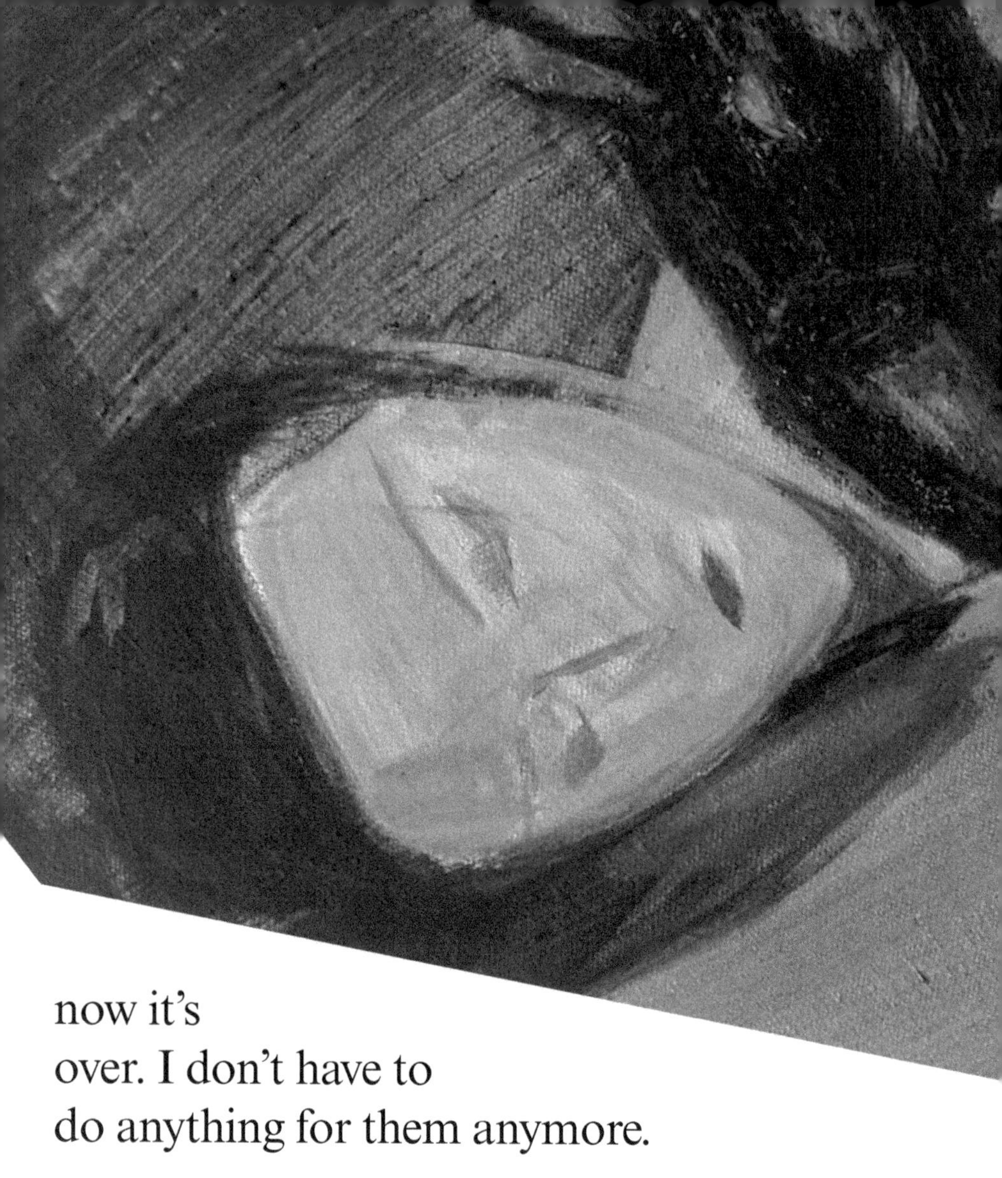

now it's
over. I don't have to
do anything for them anymore.

I know you said now you can get commissioned works, but what about other street artists? How do they make a living? Do

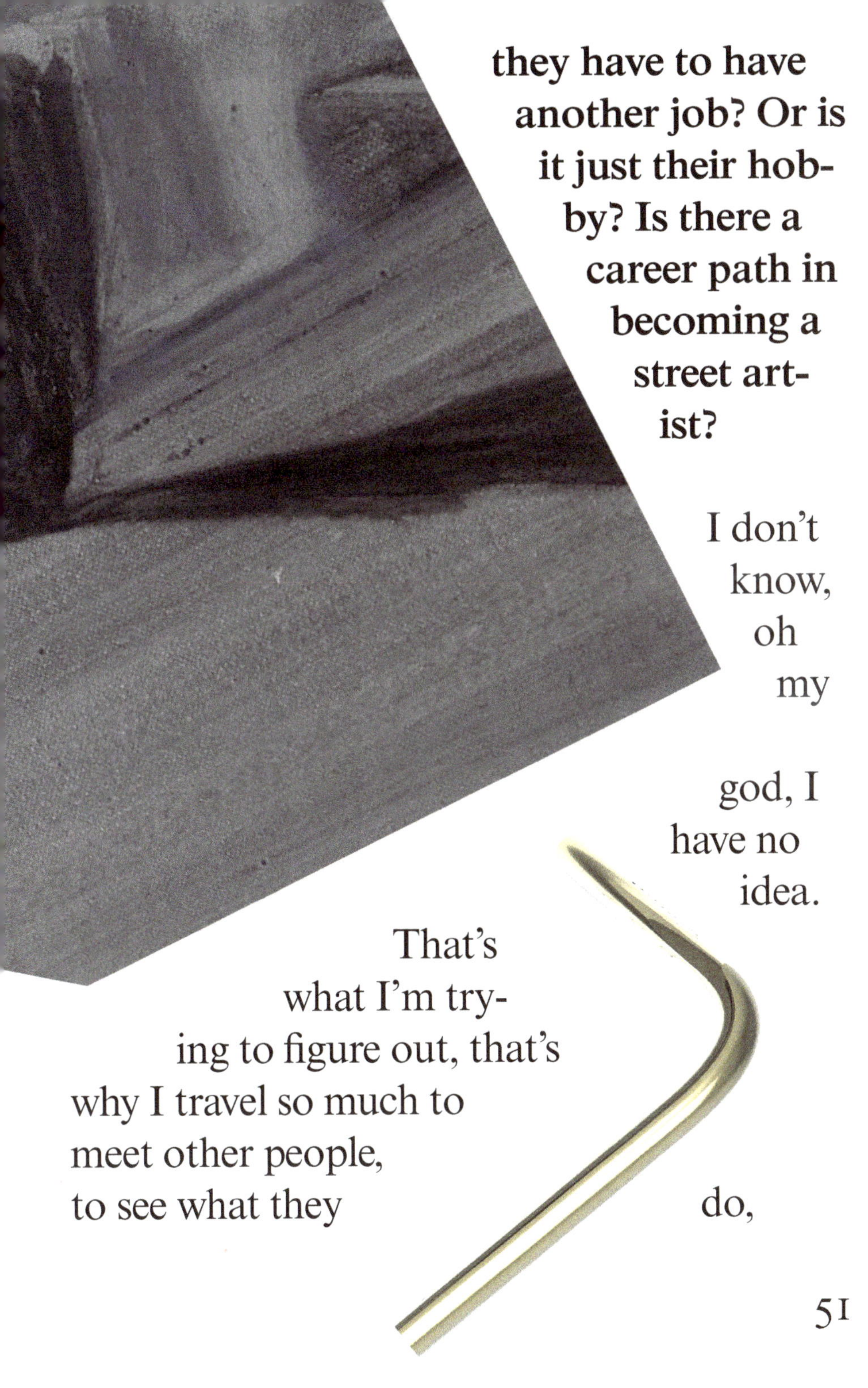

they have to have another job? Or is it just their hob-by? Is there a career path in becoming a street art-ist?

I don't know, oh my

god, I have no idea.

That's what I'm try-ing to figure out, that's why I travel so much to meet other people, to see what they do, ‘cause I have no clue. ‘Cause I don’t know where this is heading. I don’t see what the possibilities are. I’m learning so much with every trip I do. I feel in this half year my mind has been expanding so much.

Resources were very limited in Hong Kong because there was nothing. And then now I know what I want to achieve a little bit more. That’s why I have been travelling and painting nonstop now. I’m getting better and better at painting. I just want to be happy with my work, and I’m not there yet.

How and why did you start doing this?

Out of frustration.

Do you still have that?

Yes. I’m always frustrated. I think once I get comfortable, then that will be the worst. That means it’s the end. Yeah, that’s why I left Amsterdam, ‘cause it was so comfortable. Everything was perfect. It was too comfortable, I needed to go.

Don't people always seek for comfort?

Not me.

Cara，26岁，现居上海（来自比利时）

2015年1月3日
采访于上海东湖路

请先自我介绍一下？

嗨，我叫Cara Toes. 我来自比利时，我现在住在香港。我是一位街头艺术家，墙绘师。我更愿意被称作墙绘师。虽然有的人说那听上去很老派，不过我觉得这个词更好些。

叫涂鸦艺术家怎么样？

不行不行，我绝对不是涂鸦艺术家。我发现街头艺术家都不喜欢被称为涂鸦艺术家，而涂鸦艺术家也不想跟街头艺术联系在一起。

他们之间到底有什么区别？

涂鸦更多的是字母和快闪式涂鸦。而街头艺术的重点不是字母。涂鸦圈里面有很多规则。不过因为我是完全自己一个人开始做墙绘的，所以我并不了解那些历史背景性的东西。我只是想画画而已，在墙上画画。

你觉得上海怎么样？

我很喜欢这里。这挺疯狂的，因为都很偶然。不过我喜欢上海，我觉得上海是一个很酷的城市。它和香港很不一样。这里的人们都很国际化，而且我很喜欢这里即国际化，又和当地文化融合地很好。而在香港，这两个群体是很少有交集的。

你大学里是学艺术或是绘画的吗？

不是，我在亨克大学学的是生物化学。后来我又学了游戏设计。不过，我对游戏设计真的很不在行，我学它只是想要学些技术。

所以你完全是自学的绘画？

我从小就画画，不过我以为那是很正常的事情。直到我22岁，23岁的时候，我才意识到不是每个人都会画画。我小的时候一直对自己画的画觉得很不好意思，因为我觉得我画得真的很糟糕。我现在有时也还这么觉得。我在阿姆斯特丹的时候开始了一点街头艺术的创作。不过那时候我还有一份全职的工作，所以并没有很多时间。但是在香港的时候，我住的地方非常狭小，那让我非常抓狂。所以我开始每天晚上一个人到处去街上画画。那让我觉得有小小的成就感。

工作方面对你来说是什么状况？你画墙绘只是出于乐趣吗？还是你可以以此为生？

我在香港的街上画画的时候，突然有一天有个人跟我说，“哦，你画画吗？咱们一起画吧。”然后我有了一个机会参加一个很大的群展。那应该是目前为止在香港举办的最大的一个关于街头艺术的展览。因为街头艺术对香港来说还是很新鲜的事物。那个展览有非常多有名的人参加，而且有画廊的参与。我在那个展览上画了一面很大的墙，然后被画廊的人看到了。他们给了我一个个展，还介绍了一个给餐馆画墙绘的活儿。当时挺疯狂的，我花光了我最后的钱买了车票去那个餐馆，因为那里离我住的地方有点远。我花了两天时间不停地画画，最后，他们给了我钱。而正因为有了那笔钱，我才得以做了我的个展。

从那之后，很多事情就接二连三地发生了。现在，我可以经济独立。我还给Facebook在香港的办公室画了墙绘。在那之后，我有些迷茫，不知道接下来该做些什么了。你知道吗，我画了很多墙绘和现场表演。然后，在画完Facebook

的墙绘后，我突然觉得有点不知所措了。

为什么？因为给Facebook画画对你来说是一个很重要的里程碑吗？

我不会称之为里程碑。好吧，也许。一开始，我每个礼拜都很焦虑。很担心将来要找什么样的工作，我会怎么样。而后来，很多事情不停地发生了。我整个时间都非常忙碌。然后，Facebook的事发生了。我开始不知道我应该再设定怎样的目标了。在那之后，我觉得人有点空。我接了一些活儿，但是我并没有很开心。因为我发现墙绘正在慢慢地变成一份工作，而不是一件我会真心投入的事了。

所以后来，我独自去美国旅行了一个半月。那之后，我就一直在旅行，都没停过。因为我发现我非常喜欢旅行。而且当我在海外旅行的时候也能接到活。而用接活挣来的钱，我又可以继续去下一个地方旅行。我已经这样生活了半年了。

你对现在的生活满意吗？

绝对，极度，非常地满意。因为每件事都是我想要的。当我还是个小孩的时候，大概7，8岁时，我会躺在床上想，好吧，我到底想要做什么呢？我说，“嗯，我非常想要到处旅行。”那时候，我也学音乐。当你7，8岁的时候，你需要开始选择你想学习的第一件乐器。所以我就想，我应该选哪个乐器呢？我说，“好吧，也许我应该选小提琴，因为我可以到哪都带着它，我可以随便去什么地方，然后在街上拉一段挣点钱，然后继续去下一个国家，或下一个村子。”

而现在，这么多年以后，我突然意识到我已经在这么做了，不过是以更好的方式。现在这样好多了，因为墙绘可以和整个社会发生联系。在街头艺术圈，所有的人都非常友好。他们做这个是出于激情，出于乐趣。所以我们这群人，已经拥有相似的思维方式。我们不会考虑钱。没人会说他是为了钱才做这件事。我觉得很多其他的工作你会只是为了钱。而去做街头艺术却只是因为我们可以一起画画。有些艺术家甚至不说同样的语言，但我们画画，你会发现那是一种全球性的语言。

街头艺术在很多地方还都是非法的吗？你会需要躲着或是只在晚上画吗？

是啊，当然它是非法的。所以会有“Bombing”（轰炸）这样的说法。你晚上出去写下你的名字。那更多的是涂鸦。不过现在街头艺术正在被越来越多人接受。如果我看到一面墙，而我又觉得那面墙真的不错。我会问墙的主人我能不能在上面画画。这样就不违法了。我可以画一些很美丽的东西，花更多的时间在上面。因为说到底，我想要的只是做一些能改变环境的事情，并且让人们看到。

为什么你想要在外面街上的墙面上画画，而不是在工作室里的画布上画呢？

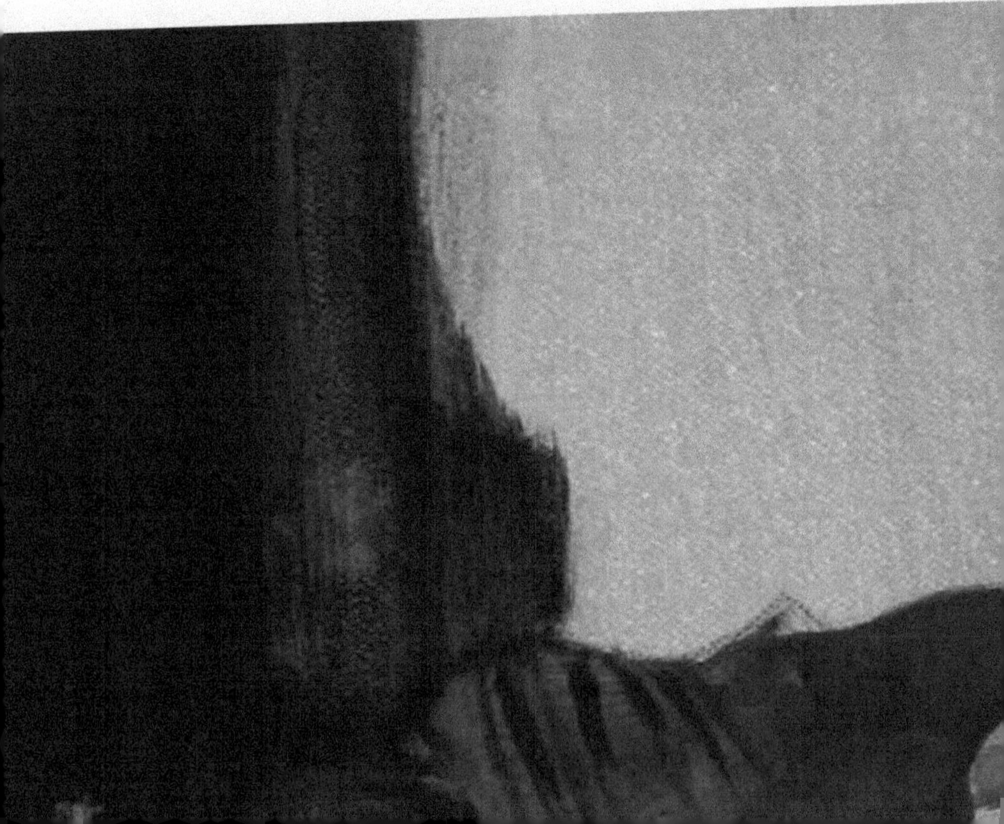

在外面画可以让更多人看到。当我在阿姆斯特丹的时候，在我骑车上班的路上，有时候我会看到一些涂鸦。然后我会觉得那些画得很烂。然后我就会想，在我骑车上班的路上，我会想要看到些什么呢？能看到一些出人意料又能改变环境的事是很有趣的。比如，哪天你看到一只吃饼干的猫什么的。

我在阿姆斯特丹的时候开始思考我小时候想要做的所有事。而且我觉得意识到你可以改变是非常重要的。你真的

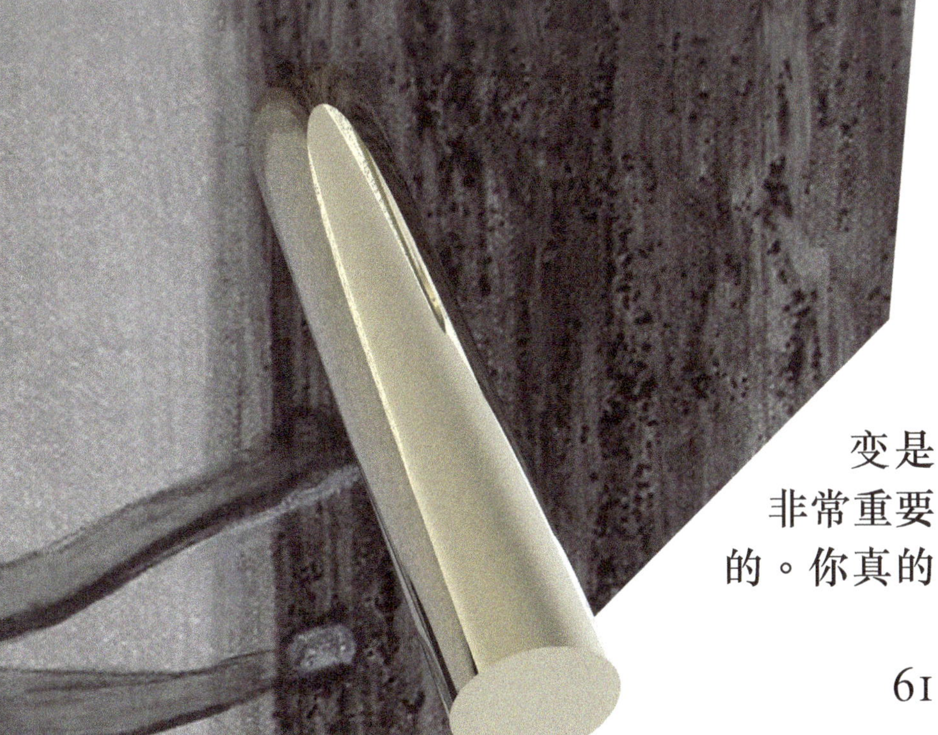

可以做你想做的任何事。因为从我的亚洲背景来说，我总是被告知我不能做我想做的事。总是做我父母想要我做的事。在我做每个决定前都会先考虑“哦，如果我这么做了我父母会怎么说？”我可不想让他们觉得丢脸。我从小是被管教地很严的。

但是在阿姆斯特丹，因为那是在另外一个国，家，我开始思考我自己到底想做什么。以前我从没想过这个问题。我之前做的每件事都是为了也许我的父母会为我骄傲，可以听到他们说，“做得不错！”

他们知道你现在在做的事吗？他们赞同吗？

现在终于是的。他们从来没有担心过我的工作或学习，因为我总是做得很好。以前，当我在学生物化学的时候，他们对那到底是什么一点概念都没有。后来我又开始学游戏设计，他们也不知道那是什么，因为他们自己从来没玩过游戏。

而墙绘是非常简单的。我只需要在墙上画画，然后拍张照片给他们看。让他们看到，哦，餐馆里，人们坐在那，我的画在墙上，这样他们就能明白。因为这非常简单。这就是做墙绘的美妙之处，人人都能明白它是什么。而且在我搬到香港以后，人们会写一些关于我的文章和访谈，那些都是中文的，所以他们可以读。然后他们就终于明白了。

Facebook的事也绝对是一个重要转折点。那时候我的父母来香港看我，我们坐在餐馆里，突然电视上就开始报道Facebook办公室里墙绘的事，所以我父母很偶然地就看到了。我自己没有电视，他们也很少看。但是在一个餐馆里，我们却一起看到了我的作品出现在电视上。所以那一刻，我意识到，好，从现在开始，我再也不需要为了他们而做什么事了。

我知道你说过你可以获得一些委托创作的工作，那么其他的街头艺术家是怎么谋生的呢？他们需要有另外的工作吗？还是街头艺术只是他们的爱好？在街头艺术圈里有所谓的职业发展道路吗？

我不知道，哦，我的天哪，我真的一点概念都没有。那是我现在正试图寻找的答案。也是为什么我做这么多旅行，去见其他的艺术家。看看他们是怎么做到的，因为我自己毫无头绪。我也不知道未来能发展成什么方向。我不知道有哪些可能性。我每次旅行都在学习很多东西。我觉得在这过去的半年里我的思维被拓展了很多很多。

在香港的时候，资源很少。因为那里真的没什么街头艺术。而我现在慢慢知道一点我想要达到什么样的目标。这也是为什么我在一直不停地旅行和画画。我现在画得越来越好了。我只是想要对自己的作品满意，但现在我还没有做到这一点。

你最初为什么想要开始到街头画画？

因为我很沮丧。

现在还会这样吗？

是啊，我总是很沮丧。我觉得哪天我真的开始觉得舒服了，那会是最糟的状况。因为那意味着一切都结束了。我之所以离开阿姆斯特丹也是因为那里太舒服了，一切都很完美。当一个地方变得太舒服的时候，我就需要离开了。

不是通常人们都会追求舒适吗？

不会是我。

www.caratoes.tumblr.com

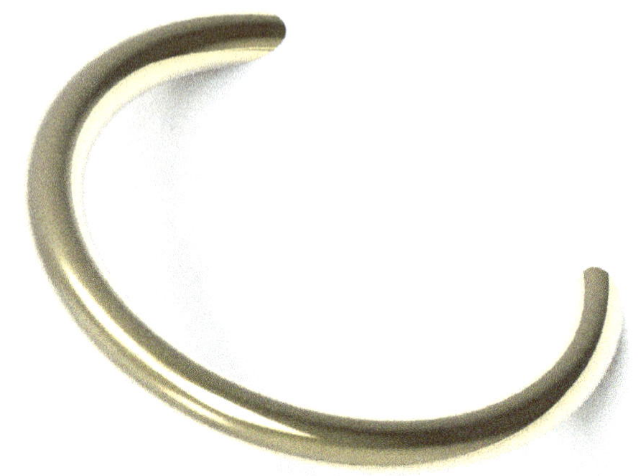

Erin, 25 years old, Berlin (From England)

Interviewed in Neukölln, Berlin
August 20th, 2015

Can you introduce yourself?

My name is *Erin*. I'm from England. I've been living in Berlin for two and a half years since graduating. I'm making art. And I have two part time jobs. One is studio manager for an artist, and the other one is–I'm a baker for a cafe.

Why did you move to Berlin?

I moved here with a friend. When we were studying I knew it wasn't an option for me to move to London, because of the cost of living. I'd been in Berlin the previous summer for a couple of months, and we just said we'd move to Berlin together after the degree. So we did.

I had no plan at all. It took me quite a long time to find my feet. Then I did an internship at a gallery for three months, and during that time, that's when I got the job with the artist *David* who I'm working for right now.

What do you have to do with the studio manager job?

Well, mainly I've been assisting *David*, (*David Thorpe*) making two large sculptures. And they are fantastic, I really love working on the sculptures. I think it's a quite unusual job for an artist assistant. If you are working with an artist, you often have to do a lot of boring jobs like shipping, organizing and online stuff. But working for *David* is really great, 'cause I'm mainly working hands-on, helping him make the sculptures, and that's really great.

I also help him with other projects, for instance I've helped him with some public sculpture commissions, and he's got a show coming up in Karlsruhe and after that in New York. He's doing lots of other projects and making works for art fairs as well, and I help him with some of the basic stuff for that too.

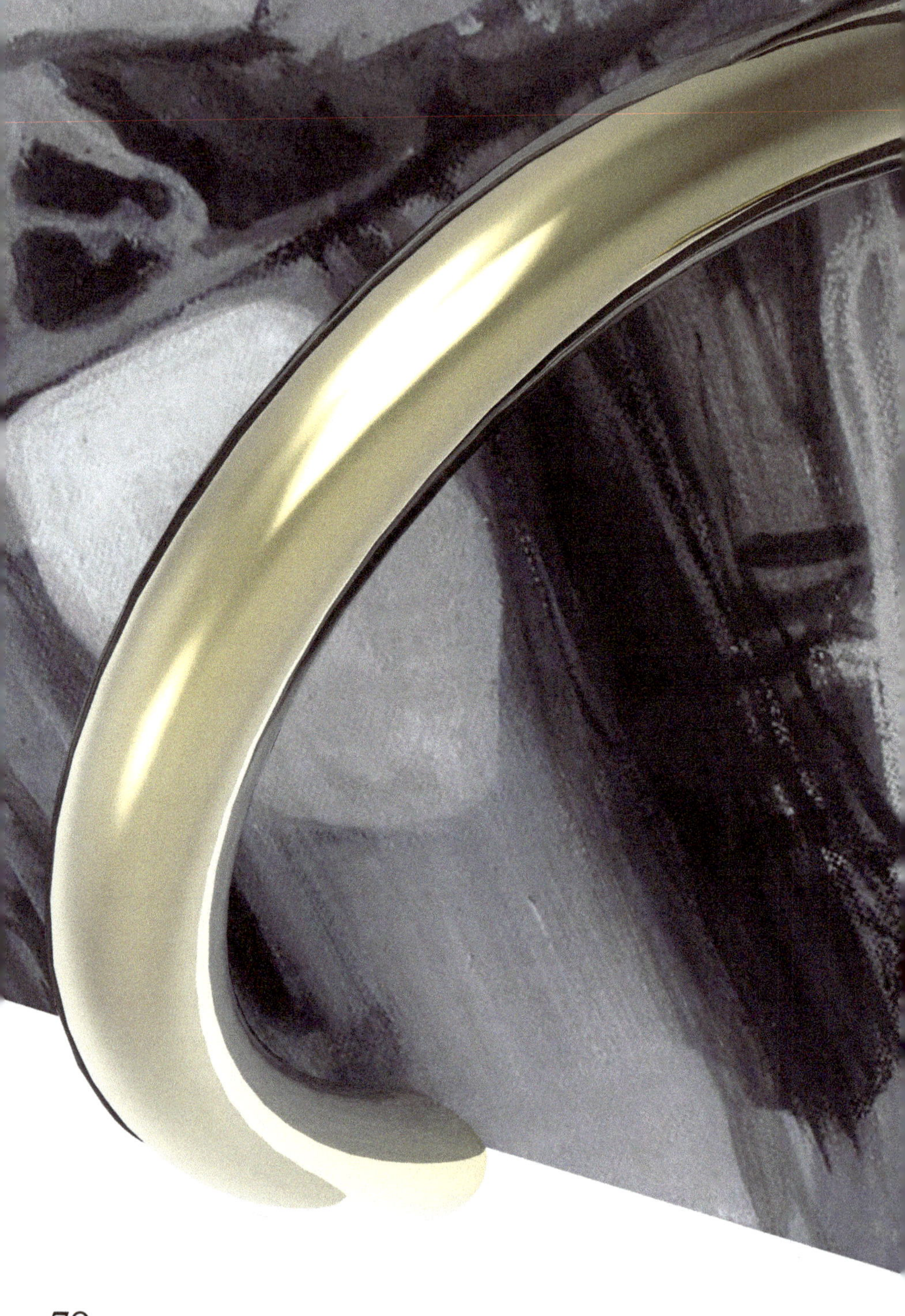

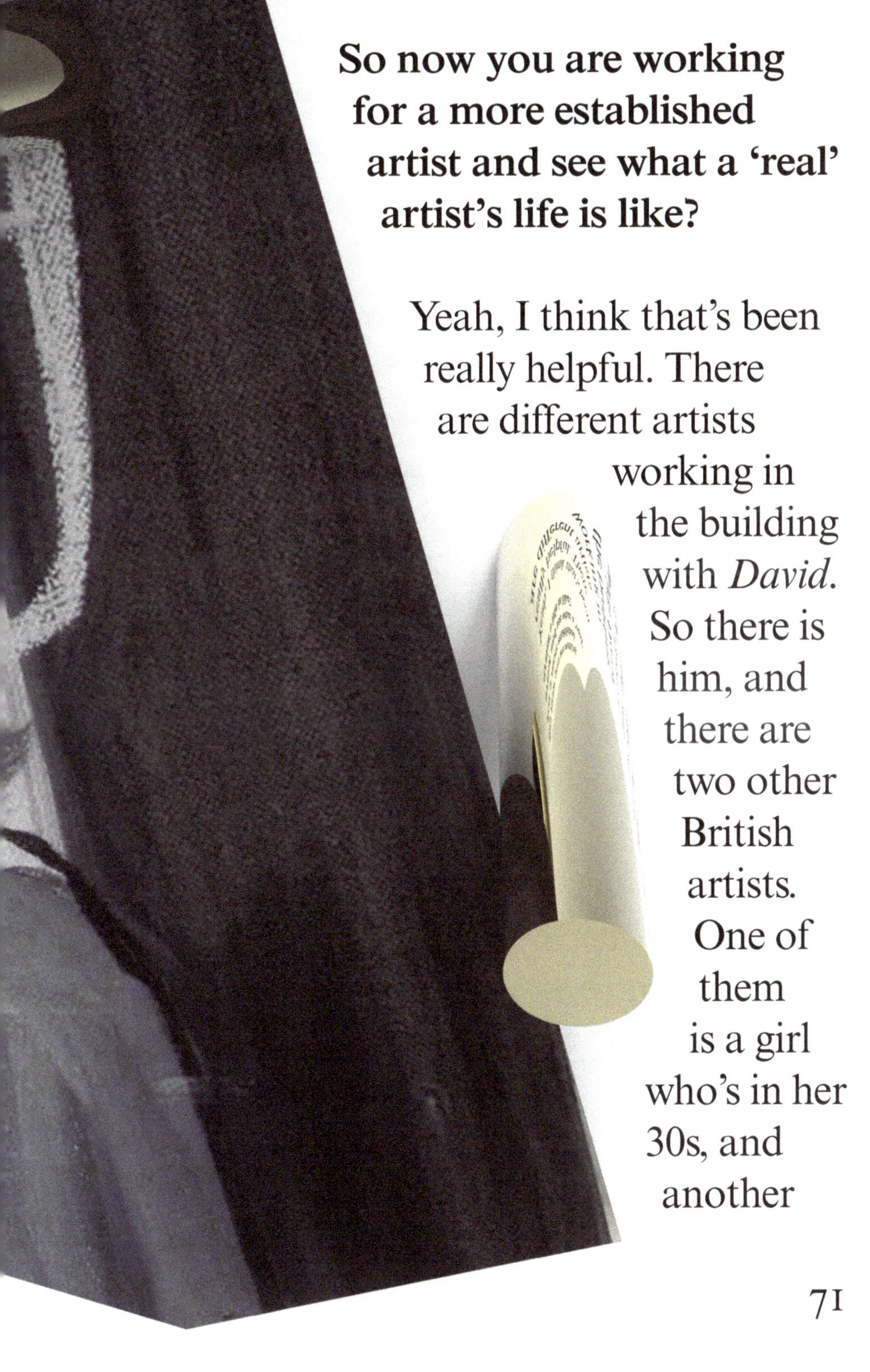

So now you are working for a more established artist and see what a 'real' artist's life is like?

Yeah, I think that's been really helpful. There are different artists working in the building with *David*. So there is him, and there are two other British artists. One of them is a girl who's in her 30s, and another guy who's also in his 30s. And there is a guy who is a little bit older and further along in his career as well. So there are different stages to be mixing around.

Is that the kind of life you want for yourself later?

I would be really really pleased.

Are those artists all living on selling their works?

Yeah. Only one of them isn't quite yet. He's starting his master's, and he had a part time job as an artist assistant for a Berlin-based artist. And the others, they are all making a living from their work. So it's quite interesting to be around these discussions.

Two of the artists there are represented by the same gallery in Berlin, one of them is having a huge solo show in New York coming up, so he's doing really well. So I do sometimes say to *David*, 'You are an artist, *David*. You are doing it. This is amazing.' He just doesn't have to do a part-time job, whereas the artists I met in London that were really established, represented by the *White Cube Gallery*, which is one of the top commercial galleries in London, were still working and teaching in 3–4 different art schools to get by.

Besides the living expense being cheaper here in Berlin, what other things are different compared to London?

The living cost difference affects a lot. I've never lived in London, but people I know that are making art in London are doing so because they've got some incredibly jammy situation.

Maybe they have a very unusually low rent, or they have parents that give them an apartment so they don't have to pay rent. Or there are also different kinds of schemes where you can get different organizations for spaces that place artists in accommodations, although the waiting list is really long. And there are some places where you can live for really really cheap rent but the contract you get is very uncertain in terms of how long you can stay there. So it's mainly like buildings that are gonna be renovated at some point in future.

But I think you would have to have some kind of other means of income.

Do your parents support or understand what you are doing here?

I think they would rather I have a more secure future. Yeah, my dad doesn't really want me to do the art. I mean they are super supportive, but they would rather 'Why don't you just have a nice job, have some kids and die? Why don't you just do that?' (Laugh)... They didn't really say that. It's more subtle than that. I'm really thankful to them though; my parents help me a lot financially in Berlin despite their concerns!

How many of your classmates after graduation decided to try life as an artist? And what was it like when you first graduated from college?

I think there were like twenty of us in our year. And I think half of the class isn't doing art anymore, and the other half still does, which is quite a high amount in our year.

It's such an exciting time when you just finish, and you are like, there is the first experience of self-sufficiency, you know, going out into the world, it's so exciting and so scary. I withdrew a lot. I think maybe being lost helps you in the long run. I don't know… but I get the impression it gets harder to carry on the older you get. It'll be interesting to see how many of my class mates are still making art in 10 or 20 years from now.

You've been here for two and half years. Do you give yourself a deadline and say maybe I'm going to try a few years more, and if my art career doesn't take off, then I'm going to do something else?

Yeah, I think it's really important to have deadlines. And things like getting my application ready for doing the master's has really helped a lot with the deadline, and wanting to do an exhibition, to have an experience to do that and to show that you are busy doing stuff, having deadlines for shows is helpful.

So I'm applying for master's courses, because I don't want to stay in Berlin much longer. I wanna be here for maybe one more year maximum, that's my Berlin deadline.

Why do you want to leave Berlin?

Because I feel that it was a really really great

place to come straight after undergraduate. It's given me the chance to think about what I want to make, what I want to do. The city has such a slow pace of life. Even the streets are wider. There is so much more space to think. And I think this has really helped me a lot.

But I'm kind of conscious that if I want to make this art career happen, then I need to jump into something more challenging and fast-paced. I think I could make it work here, but for me, Berlin is just about having more time. I don't want to place myself here as a professional artist. I wanna situate myself in a different place. But for me Berlin was about breathing time and working in a studio, meeting people, working stuff out.

So you think going back to school for a master's degree will help with this artistic career?

Yeah, I think so. I think it will. It should.

After that, if I don't get anywhere after the master's, that's when I can start panicking!

Is it like if you want to be a real artist, nowadays you have to have a master's degree?

No, it's not true. You don't have to. You don't have to at all if you are really well-connected already. Or if you are in a good place already, you will get seen. And I think a master's can offer that exposure. A master's can also be a really good time to focus on your work and have all the facilities as well. Things like that can really open a lot. There is so much more I have to learn about, practicing and getting feedback. I just think it would be really really fun as well.

How many days in a week do you come to work in the studio, and how many days do you spend working for your money job?

Well, I work about 4 days a week on my own art, 3 afternoon shifts for *David*, normally, and one morning shift a week in a cafe. It's good to do something that's totally outside the art bubble. I've been helping *David* with these two sculptures for two years, and we are about a third of the way through. It's nice to go at such a slow pace in the thinking progress, but it's also nice to go to the café where you make a cake and it's done, then you make another one. That's also quite satisfying.

So you like the balance?

I like the balance at the moment, I do. Even though friends of mine are saying 'Quit the bakery, that's bullshit, it's such a waste of time.' But now I've cut my hours down to just one day a week. And I think for me, that's fine. When I go to the bakery, I always think I can go to the studio afterwards. But every time I work in the bakery, I haven't come to the studio and had those good hours working

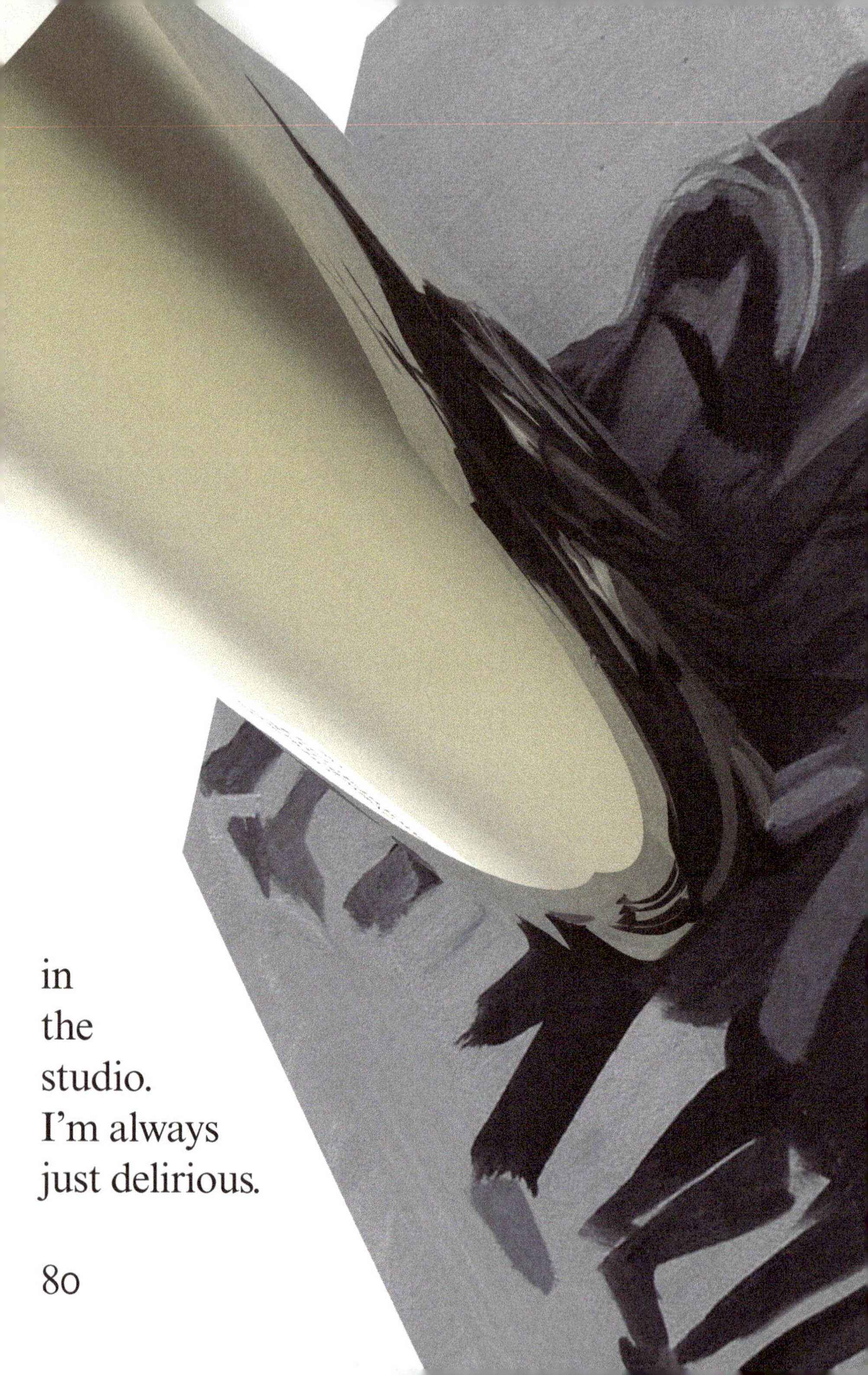

in
the
studio.
I'm always
just delirious.

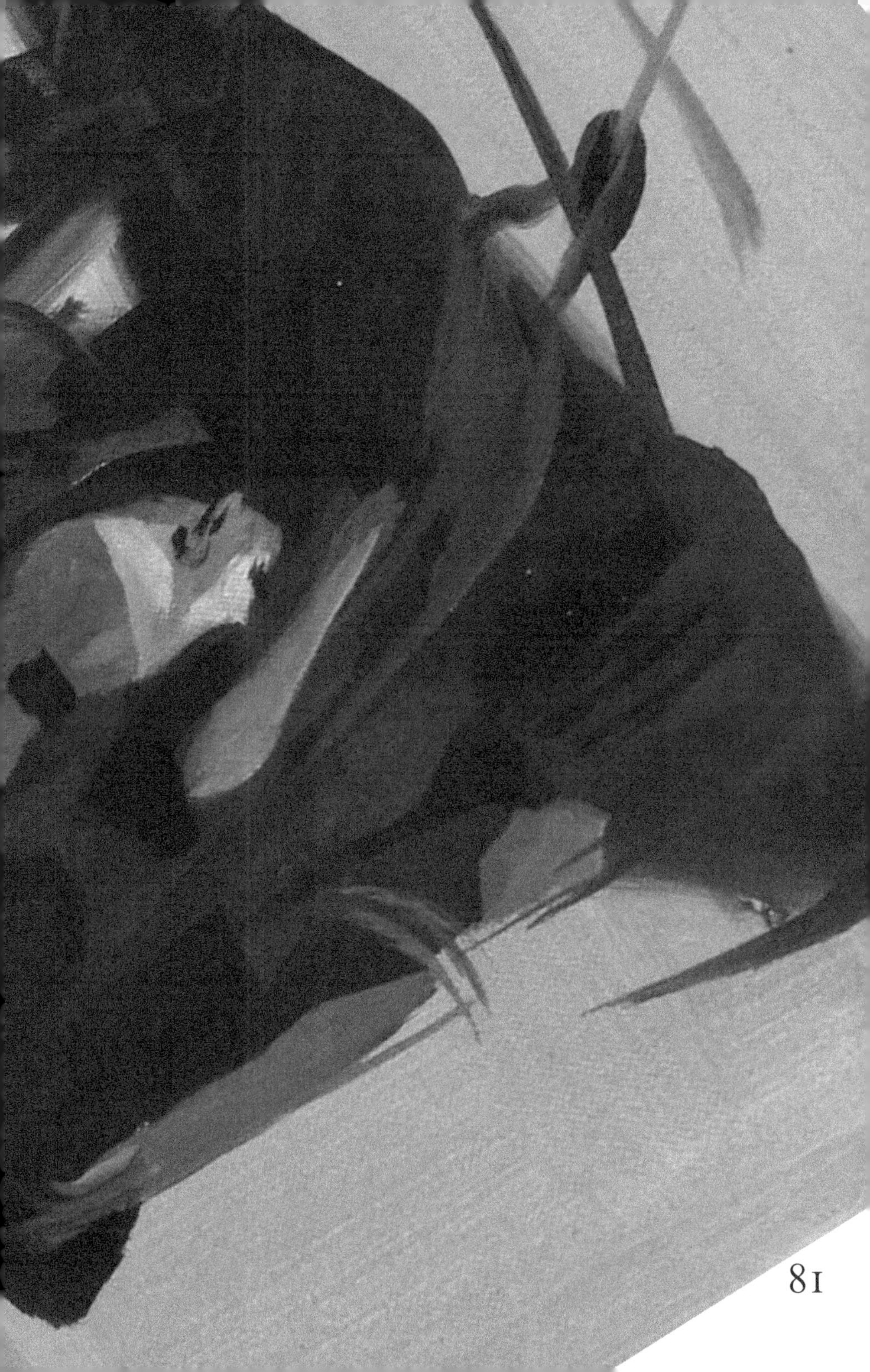

Are you able to pay your cost of living here with the part time jobs you have?

Yeah. The two part time jobs I have give me about 1100 Euros. I was also doing other random stuff as well. Like I was giving art lessons to kids. I was baking cakes for local cafes around Neukölln. So yeah, if you want more money, you can do that, that's enough for me to survive. And then I get help from my dad as well, still. I'm saving that extra help for the master's next year, 'cause London is going to be very different.

What's the basic living cost here in Berlin?

At the moment, I think you can live very comfortably on a thousand Euros a month. I mean I have been paying for my studio with 170 euros, and my apartment is around 380 euros a month. So around 600 euros for rent. You can have 100 euros a week for food and going out.

I guess it's a good thing that there are so many artists and creative people living here in Berlin so you really get that sense of community. But does that also make you feel less special since you are just one of them?

Yeah, there is a bit of that definitely. But I think that doesn't come to the surface that often for me. Maybe because the openings and stuff that I've been going to, there is very much a sort of expat community. And I see the same faces there all the time, and it's only when I step outside of this small circlet, then I'm like 'Oh my god!'

There is UDK, the art school in Berlin. They have a HUGE party every year, and I had a really weird feeling there. There's just thousands of young, good-looking hipsters or young creatives, thousands and thousands of them. All these people. And I'm like, who are these people? I haven't seen any of these faces before. It was really overwhelming and I had to sit down. It's too much.

I think there are different bubbles of art communities in Berlin and everywhere. For instance, the openings I go to, I barely hear Germen being spoken. I just hear American, Canadian accents. And I'm like, where is this German art scene? And my friend was telling me that the German artists here feel quite hurt that there is this expat community, these American and Canadians get visas for a couple of years and they come here with this mission to network the fuck out of it and do their projects, and those are the things that get written about in a lot of the magazines. And there is this German community… it's like a different world, because there is such a huge influx of people from America and Canada, they come together in groups, and they just form this separate bubble. It's strange.

Why do you feel like you want to be an artist?

Well, I grew up in a small conservative town in the South on England. So I think it's easy to get excited when you start hearing stories about SOHO, and London in the 80s. This idea of bohemia where like gays mixing with straight, and there is no gender going on and there is no class going on, poor people mixing with aristocrats, all sorts of things and it's all based on what you have to say. This magical idea of bohemia that is so appealing and seductive.

Coming from this very conservative town, it's like, I want to be around people that are nuts, I want to be around people that are thinking about things. And that was the initial pull for me. I felt very much like an outsider. You have this idea that there is a place where you can do whatever you want and be whoever you want, all these kind of wonderful ideas.

I can also see that I was probably influenced by my high school. I felt it wasn't cool to be clever but it was socially acceptable to be good at drawing and painting. It's getting better now but these are the sort of biases that you pick up on as a young person. The same reason there just aren't as many female engineers for example. So I think I was probably influenced by trying to fit in but I was competitive in art. I had this weird drive for making stuff. I found it hard but exciting and I felt really driven.

And then I went to art school, I didn't have ideas about art or what art was, or any idea of art history at all. And I still have huge gaps of culture, theory and these kinds of things. But that was when I got introduced to those ideas. I think the more and the further along that you go down this route, the more you have a clear idea of what it is.

What's your clearer idea about art now? Is it as bohemian as you thought?

In a lot of ways, I think I was a bit surprised. I didn't go to openings that much before I moved to Berlin. And at the openings you see certain people that are good in these social situations being very professional and having this social power, and how that is like, important. And that's a whole side of being an artist that really wasn't part of what I thought I would have to do. And I think maybe I don't have to worry about these social power games. But I guess it was the first time that I was being made aware of it.

Seems like nowadays to be a professional artist, only making good artworks is not enough, you also have to be informed with art history/art theory, being intelligent and able to talk about your work. You also need studio management skills and social networking abilities.

You don't have to, you could just work on your art and maybe get discovered when you're dead or become an outsider artist. But you still need an income to do even that! I believe that most artists develop those business skills in order to have a better chance of earning money from their work, ultimately so they have more time in the studio. So I don't knock it. It's just annoying when artists, or anyone connected to the arts, appear to be driven only by social hierarchies, doing drugs with the right people to get ahead, or social climbing. That can actually work for a period of time but it seems to me that for a long-term success artists tend to have some combination of business-like skills. The difficulty is that artists have become more and more refined in these skills and it sadly takes energy away from your practice in order to compete. For me, right now I try not to think about all that too much, I just need to be in the studio more.

But if you are only making art in your

studio and no one knows about it…

I mean, you can just be in your studio, and maybe a curator's car breaks down and they knock on the door, and you are the only person around. (Laugh) But I don't wanna do that. I don't really want to be friends with important people that will push my career. I wanna be talking to people in this way, with other artists and give this 'art thing' a bloody good go. That would be ideal.

Erin quit the bakery job and is preparing to start her Master's study at Royal Academy of Arts in London in the autumn.

Erin，25岁，现居柏林（来自英国）

2015年8月20日
采访于柏林Neukölln

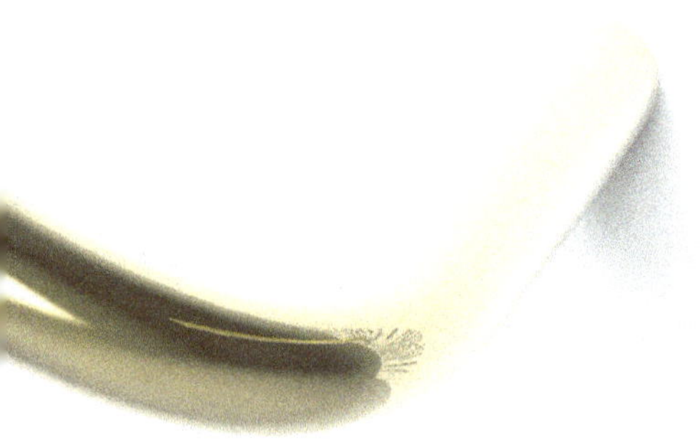

你可以自我介绍一下吗？

我叫Erin，我来自英国。从毕业后搬来柏林到现在我已经在这生活了2年半时间了。我做艺术。另外我还有两份兼职的工作。一个是给艺术家管理工作室，另一个是在咖啡馆做烘培师。

你为什么搬来柏林？

我是和一个朋友一起搬过来的。当我还在上学的时候我就知道去伦敦生活对我来说是不现实的，因为生活成本太高了。我在之前的夏天来柏林呆过几个月。所以我跟我的朋友就说，等我们拿到文凭后就搬来柏林。所以我们就来了。

我一开始一点计划儿都没有。花了很长时间才找到一点方向。后来我在一个画廊做了3个月实习。就是在那段时间，我找到了现在这份给艺术家David工作的活儿。

你帮艺术家管理工作室都需要做些什么呢？

我主要在帮David做两个大型雕塑。我非常喜欢做雕塑。我觉得这份工作挺不常见的。通常如果给艺术家做助理会需要做很多无聊的运输、组织管理和网络方面的工作。但是给David工作非常棒，因为他会让你真的动手去做。像我现在就在帮他做雕塑，这真的很棒。

他现在在做一些委托创作的公共雕塑和几个其他的项目。然后马上会在卡尔斯鲁厄和纽约做展览。另外还要给艺博会做作品。我也帮他做那些项目的基本工作。

所以你现在给一个已经比较有名的艺术家工作并且可以看到一个"真正的艺术家"的生活是怎样的？

对，我觉得这方面的帮助对我还是挺大的。我们所在的楼里还有很多其他艺术家。除了David以外，还有另外两个英国艺术家。其中有一位30多岁的女生，还有另外一个男生也是30多岁。另外还有一个男生年纪要稍大些，并且职业生涯也发展地更进一步。所以我可以看到很多不同职业阶段艺术家的状态。

所以那样的生活是你以后想要的吗？

如果可以的话，我会非常非常开心。

所以那些艺术家都能靠卖作品为生吗？

是的。只有其中一位还没有，他正要开始去上研究生。他之前也有过一份给其他艺术家当助理的兼职工作。但是其他的人全都能靠卖作品生活。所以能听到关于这些的讨论还挺有意思的。

他们中间有两位艺术家被柏林的同一家画廊代理。其中一位马上会在纽约有一个非常大的个展，所以他混得挺不错的。我有时会跟David说，“Daivd，你是个艺术家哎。你真的成为艺术家了，这太棒了！”他完全不需要另一份兼职的工作。而我在伦敦认识的，也已经很有建树，而且已经被白立方画廊代理了的艺术家却还要做另外的工作，靠在3–4个不同艺术学校教书来勉强度日。要知道白立方已经是伦敦最顶尖的商业画廊之一了。

除了这里的生活成本相对便宜以外，柏林还有哪些方面和伦敦相比较起来会有所不同呢？

生活成本的差异造成的影响还挺大的。我从来没真的在伦敦生活过。但是我所认识的在伦敦做艺术的人之所以能这么做都是因为他们有令人难以置信的优越处境。

或者他们有低到非常不正常的房租，要不就是他们的父母给了他们一个公寓，所以他们不需要付房租。或者还有一些其他的办法。比如，你可以从一些帮助艺术家寻找住所的机构那里找到空间。尽管他们的候选名单非常长。另外还有些地方房租非常非常便宜，但是你能拿到的合同却极其不确定你到底能在那里呆多久。基本上那些都是将来不知道哪天就会需要重新整修的大楼。

不过我觉得你总是会需要有一些其他方面的收入。

你的父母支持或理解你在这儿做的事吗？

我觉得他们更希望我有个更加有安全感的未来。我爸并不真的希望我做艺术。尽管他们都很支持我，但是他们更倾向于，“为什么你不找个好工作，生几个孩子然后死去呢？”（笑）他们并没有真的那么说。我还是挺感激他们的。尽管他们很为我担心，但是我在柏林的生活他们在经济方面还是给了我很多帮助。

你的同学当中有多少毕业后决定要尝试当艺术家的？你刚毕业的时候情况是怎样的？

我们那一届大概有20个人。我觉得班里有一半人都已经没有再做艺术了。而另一半还在做着。其实比例还挺高的。

刚毕业的时候是挺让人兴奋的。那是你第一次开始需要尝试自给自足，面对世界。所以那挺让人振奋但也挺让人害怕。我一开始常常退缩。我觉得也许迷失一阵对以后长期来说是有帮助的。我也不确定。但是我感觉年纪越大越不容易继续下去。我也很好奇10年或20年以后我和我的同学们还有多少人仍然在做艺术。

你会不会给自己设置一个截止日期说，“我会再尝试几年，如果那时我的职业艺术生涯还没有起步，那我就去做点别的？”

是的。我觉得有截止日期非常重要。比如准备申请研究生的截止日期，想要做展览，获得做展览的经历，以及让人看到你在忙着做事，有个做展览的截止日期什么的都挺有帮助的。

所以我正在申请研究生课程，因为我不想在

柏林再呆更久了。我会在这里再最多呆上一年。这是我给柏林的截止日期。

为什么你想要离开柏林？

我觉得柏林是一个非常适合刚毕业之后过来呆一阵的城市。它给了我思考到底要做什么的机会。这个城市的生活节奏很慢。连街道都要宽阔些。有很多空间留给人去思考。我觉得这对我帮助很大。

但是我有点担心如果我想要让我的艺术生涯真的发生，那我得要换到一个更具挑战性，节奏更快的地方。我不想在这里做职业艺术家。对我来说，柏林是关于呼吸的时间，在工作室里做作品，遇见其他人，以及尝试各种事情。

所以你觉得回学校念研究生会对你的艺术生涯有帮助？

是的。我觉得是这样。应该是这样。在那之后，如果我研究生毕业了艺术方面还是没有什么起色，那时候我就该开始恐慌了。

是不是这年头如果要做个“真正的艺术家”，就必须要拿到研究生文凭？

不，这不是真的。不一定要这样。也许你根本不需要。如果你已经有广泛的人脉。或是如果你已经发展地不错，那你会被注意到的。而我觉得研究生学位可以为你提供这些条件。研究生阶段的学习也是非常好的可以让你专注于自己的作品的时间，你还会有使用各种器材的机会。这样的环境可以为你打开很多可能性。我还有很多东西要学习，以及获得反馈。而且这会是一段非常快乐的时光。

一周里面你有几天会来工作室工作？又有几天需要用来做挣钱的工作？

我一周会有四天时间用来做自己的作品。然后有三个下午给艺术家David工作，另外一天在咖啡馆上早班。我觉得有时候做些和艺术完全无关的事情也挺好的。我帮David做这两个雕塑已经有两年了，而我们才完成了大概三分之一的进度。能以这么慢的速度来边想边做事非常好。但是去咖啡馆一会儿就做完一个蛋糕，然后再接着做另一个。那也挺让人有满足感的。

所以你喜欢这样的平衡？

目前我喜欢这样的平衡，没错。尽管我的朋友们劝我辞掉咖啡馆的工作，说那是浪费时间。我已经减少我的工作时间到一周只去一天了。对我来说这没有问题。虽然每次去完烘培店后，我都以为可以过来工作室再工作一会儿。但是每次都没有做到。我总是不在状态。

你能靠你的兼职工作负担每个月在这里的生活开销吗？

是的。我的两份兼职工作能给我大概1100欧的收入。我同时也总还做些其他乱七八糟的活儿。比如我给小朋友上艺术课。我还给Neukölln当地的咖啡店做蛋糕。所以如果你真的想要多挣钱的话，你是可以做那些的。那也已经足够我生活了。另外我爸也会再给我些钱。但是我准备把那些钱存起来留着明年上研究生时用。

现在柏林的最基本生活成本是多少？

目前，我觉得你每个月有1000欧就可以生活地很舒服。比如我每个月付170欧来租工作室。我的公寓是每个月大约380欧。所以房租一共加起来需要大概600欧。你可以每周再留100欧用于食物和外出。

我猜一方面柏林有这么多艺术家和创意人士在这里生活是好事，因为你真的会有社群感。但是会不会这样也会让你觉得自己不够特别，因为你只是这么多人中的又一个？

是的。肯定有这方面因素。但是好在我并不太经常明显感觉到这一点。也许因为我去的那些开幕式大都是外国人的群体。我总是看到同样的那几张面孔。只有当我踏出这个小圈子的时候才会突然觉得“哦，我的天哪！”

柏林有个学校叫UDK（柏林艺术大学）。他们每年都有一个超级大的派对。我上次去的时候有过非常奇怪的感觉。当时有成百上千的年轻又长得好看的文艺青年和创意人士。成千上万！那么多人。我就在想，他们都是谁啊？我以前从来没见过这些人。太让人受不了了。我不得不坐下。

我觉得不管是在柏林还是在其他任何地方，都存在着不同的封闭的艺术小圈子。比如，我会去参加的那些开幕式就很少会听到有人说德语。我只听到美国口音和加拿大口音的英语。我就在想，传说中的德国艺术圈到底在哪呢？我的朋友跟我说这里的德国艺术家因为这些外国艺术家的社群而觉得挺受伤害的。因为这些美国和加拿大的艺术家们拿了几年的签证，带着要充分利用一切社交资源和做艺术项目的决心来到这里。他们所做的经常被很多媒体杂志报道。而德国艺术家的社群，那就好像是另一个世界。因为有太多人从美国和加拿大成群结伴地涌来这里，他们在这里形成了自己隔离的小圈子。还挺奇怪的。

你为什么觉得想要做艺术家？

我在英国南部一个保守的小镇长大。所以很容易当你听到关于SOHO和八十年代伦敦的故事的时候会很激动。同性恋和异性恋混杂在一起，没有性别和阶级的存在，穷人和贵族混杂在一起等等，完全取决于你到底有什么要说的。这样魔幻的波西米亚式想法非常吸引人和具有诱惑性。

我来自一个非常保守的小镇。但我想要和疯

狂的人在一起。我想要身边都是思考问题的人。所以那是艺术最初吸引我的原因。我觉得自己像个外来者。想象着有这么一个地方我可以做任何想做的事，做我想做的人。所有类似这样的美妙的想法。

还有可能因为在我高中的时候，我觉得聪明不是一件很酷的事，而对画画在行却似乎更容易被社会接受。当你还很年轻的时候是很容易被周围的环境影响的。再加上我也很喜欢做东西。我觉得它非常难但又非常令人兴奋。让人充满了动力。

后来我上了艺术学校，那时我还完全没有艺术和艺术史的任何概念。即使是现在我也还有很多关于文化，理论和相关方面的知识空缺。我觉得你沿着这个方向走得越远，就会越清楚艺术到底是什么。

你现在对艺术有更清晰的想法了吗？它还是像你一开始想象的那样波西米亚吗？

在很多方面，我想现实都是有些出乎我的意料的。在搬来柏林之前，我没有很常去开幕式。而在开幕式的时候，你会看到有些人在那类社交环境中非常在行，如鱼得水，非常专业，他们具有这种社交能力。而那似乎是很重要的。但那是关于艺术家，我真的没想到过需要去做的部分。我觉得也许我并不需要去担心这些社交权力游戏。但是我猜那是我第一次意识到了这件事的存在。

似乎今天要做一名职业艺术家，仅仅做好的作品还不够，你需要了解艺术史，艺术理论，要足够聪明并且能谈论自己的作品，还要有管理工作室的技巧和社交的能力。

我并不觉得你一定这么做，你也可以就只是一个人做作品，直到你死了才会被人发现。或者变成外围艺术家。但即使是这样你也需要收入来生活呀。我相信大多数的艺术家训练出那些生意的技能只是为了获得更好地通过他们的作品来挣钱的机会。最终，他们只是想花更多时间在工作室里创作。所以我不会说那样不好。只是有时候真的很烦看到有些艺术家或是和艺术相关的人士，他们似乎只是把攀爬社会等级当作动力，通过和对的人一起嗑药来上位。那样也许短期会奏效吧。我觉得长期来看，一个成功的艺术家似乎确实需要有些生意方面的技能。问题只是在于，当艺术家这方面的技能越来越好的时候，很多创作的精力却被消耗了。对我来说，我现在尽量不太去考虑这些问题。我就是需要花更多时间在工作室里做作品。

但是如果你只是在工作室里做你的艺术，却没人知道你的作品怎么办？

我是说，你当然可以只是在工作室里呆着，然后也许某个策展人的车坏了，他不得不来敲你的门，因为周围就没有别的人可以帮忙了。（笑）但是我不想要那样。我并不真的想要通过和重要的人做朋友来推进我的事业。我想要和其他人，其他艺术家，就像现在我们这样地聊天，并努力地去尝试做艺术。那就够理想的了。

Erin辞掉了面包房的工作。目前正在为秋季开始在英国皇家艺术学院的研究生学习做准备。

Francois, 32 years old, Berlin (From France)

Interviewed at Berlin, Prinzessinengarten
August 3rd, 2015

Can you please introduce yourself?

I'm *Francois*. I'm from Bretagne in France. It's a really good part of France. I was beginning my art study over there before I came to Berlin, and then I started to make a lot of exchange studies in Germany. I studied for my bachelor's degree in art history, culture and cultural science in different places. After that, I studied at *École des Beaux-Arts* in Paris for 4 years and got my diploma there. Then I went for my Master's in Berlin, but I didn't finish because it was boring. I had so much in my head, it was time to stop and to make something with my life.

How long have you been in Berlin?

I'm in and out in Berlin. If I add all my time in Berlin together, it would be 3 years minimum. But this time I've been here for one year, and I'll go back soon to France.

I don't want to spend another winter here, I don't want to.

What are you going to do in France?

I don't know. I will be between my home place in Bretagne and in Paris. I have a project in September in Paris with an artist friend who invited me. Then in October, I have another project in Strasbourg.

I hate this word 'project', but I have to use it sometimes. I am the artist who doesn't want to speak about the project. I don't want to do applications. I do it sometimes because I don't know what to do to get in, but I don't want to get in. That's the problem.

Why?

Because I don't like the style of how they do it. I like art. I make art. I like to exhibit. I want to exhibit. But I don't like the art game and I don't want to play the game.

So what kind of art do you do?

I make video installations. That was the focus for my diploma, and that's my research. The starting point is the working artist, the artist who uses his body to connect to art. First, I did a lot of research that was at a time when I was not an artist but someone who was studying art history.

What's your definition of an artist?

I don't have one. I guess a free man who wants to bring something to the people and who has a real interest in doing something creative that can change the world. We have different kinds of weapons. But if you want to be an artist, you have to decide if you use this weapon.

For example, when I was making videos, I wanted tools that are modern. So I didn't make paintings, because I wanted to use the tools that my enemy, the mass media also use. Because if I want to say something about it I have to use the same medium.

I was not a computer freak. I didn't watch TV when I was a kid. I had my first computer when I was 22. So I had to learn all the techniques, but I was used to images and learned to analyze it.

First, I understand how to analyze an image. And then, I go into it to make a video to say something about it. I use little camera movement. I have just a tripod and I'm alone, having no team. Like a painter, but I'm with my camera.

Do you have a website for your work?

I really don't like this Internet stuff. But I have a Vimeo account, which is a platform like Youtube but a little bit more professional in a way, and protected also, respectful for what you do.

Why do you not like the Internet?

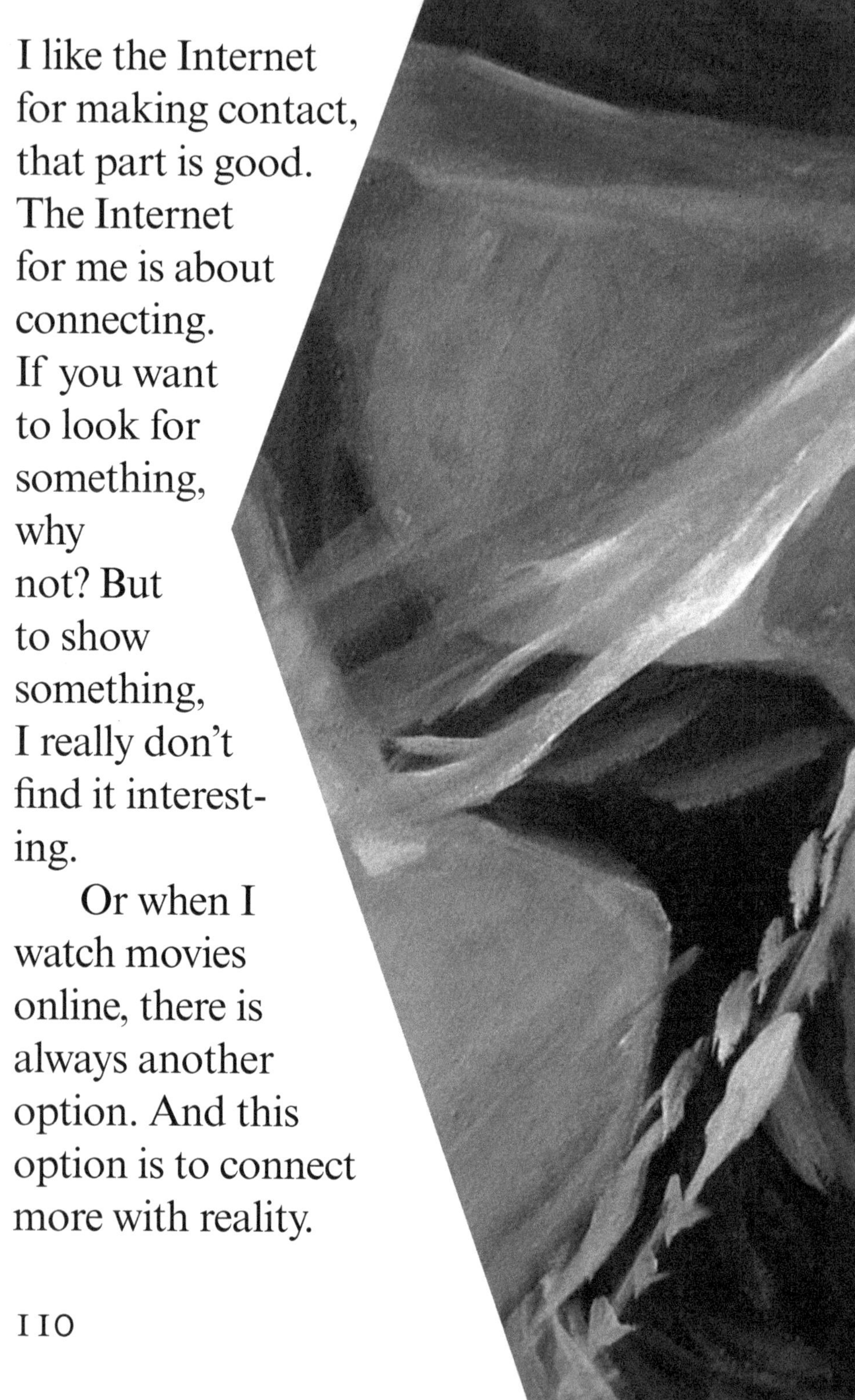

I like the Internet for making contact, that part is good. The Internet for me is about connecting. If you want to look for something, why not? But to show something, I really don't find it interesting.

Or when I watch movies online, there is always another option. And this option is to connect more with reality.

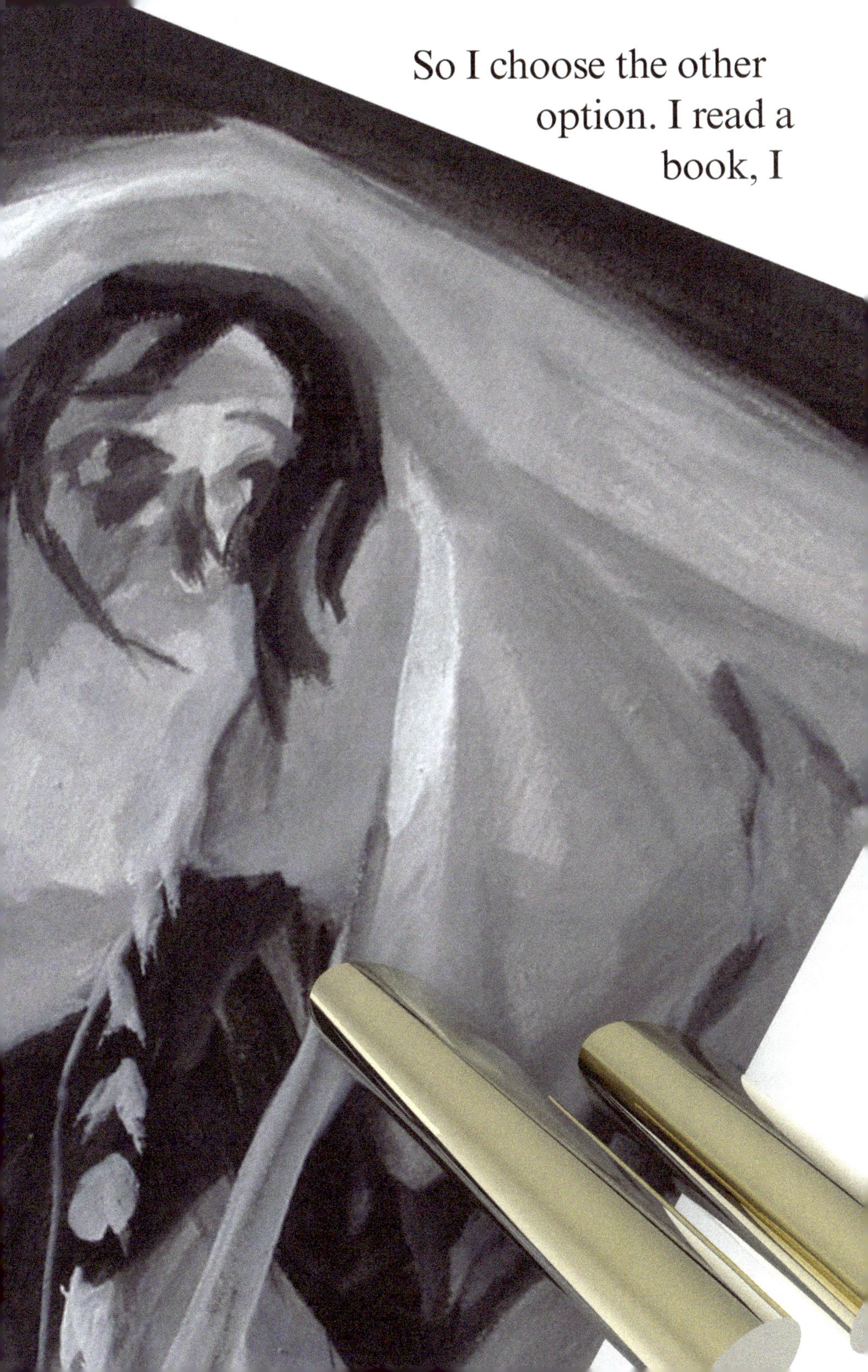

So I choose the other
option. I read a
book, I

go to the cinema, I meet a girl instead of going to Youporn. Actually, it's better. I try to do it the real way, because then you lose yourself in this infinity of possibility.

Ok, what people show on the Internet, they already show somewhere else. So I prefer to go where they show in reality. I don't need that. I have so many opportunities to make, to meet people and to exchange really, stuff in the eyes.

How is life for you in Berlin?

It's really comfortable and big here. There are not so many people and it's a huge place. I'm now living in Wedding which is a little bit of an upcoming area.

I'm always in the upcoming places. The first time I came here, and that was about 8–10 years ago, that time I was living in Prenzlauer Berg, and that was the end of the good time. Then it was the gentrification.

Gentrification is a process. Now it's

happening at Mobbit. I'm part of it, I'm part of the gentrification. Artists are in the center of this process. They discover the new place, then they make a little bar or other nice little things, then they tell their friends to come. Then the investment starts. The money-makers, the builders comes after, and make money. Then they make the place expensive and slowly push people out.

Do you think there are too many artists in Berlin?

I don't care. I really don't care.

Really? Do you think it's nicer to have this community around you?

It's random. But all my friends are artists. Most of my friends are kind of connected with art and do art. This is my life. It's normal. I meet people who share the same life ideas and stuff. My friends are artists.

But I'm not into the art scene. I don't go to the gallery. I don't go to the museum often. I was doing it when I was studying, because it was my job to study. But now, it's over.

So you are just doing your own thing? You don't care what's happening in the so-called art world?

I really don't care. But I have my eyes open. I see things even when I don't go. I'm an intelligent guy. I don't have to go and show my face to understand what's happening. Because I know, I studied that all my life, I know all the tricks. I do my work. I try to find and connect with other artists and communities which are doing similar things like me, which is not trendy, but making things interdisciplinary. I made a woodshop and say it's actually art.

For you, is being an artist or making art actually a way of living, instead of getting

professionalized in this gallery or museum art world direction?

It's not bad if I have museums or galleries inviting me. I would say yes for sure.

Are you trying to go that direction? Are you making an effort?

I try to be myself and to stay myself. I don't want to make stuff so they will accept me. I don't want to think about what they want. Because if I just start to do that, then I will lose myself, I will lose my creativity. I will lose my art. Maybe I will have them, but, what the fuck, I don't want them.

Artists are just tools for them. 'Them' being museums, galleries, and curators. They make their names bigger than the artists. They say they organize the stuff. They make a dream team of artists, then they take control. And then we are just pieces of what they need to reach to the point they want to reach, which is a lot of recognition and money.

They don't choose me for example, because they know I will criticize it. So they only choose the artists that are willing to play their game. Because these kinds of artists they don't want to do art, they want to make money. And they think, why not be an artist, because everyone can be an artist.

I want to have the world, and to have my self-confidence, my pleasure. Anyway, maybe I don't care. Maybe I will be known in 200 years. If what I'm doing is good for the world, then it's good. If it's not interesting, it's not interesting.

I like to think about big things. So, the little gallery world, the little contemporary art, the little stuff… I stay out of that, but I know the direction, because I studied it. So I don't answer my own question, I answer the question of time, in art history. And we are now at the point where there are these questions that need to be answered, so there are some artists that need to answer these questions, now.

What are those questions?

Interdisciplinary. Mixing stuff, mixing all different arts and people. To make people understand that it's a little bit more complicated than just to make an art piece and be an artist.

It's not like you make an art piece and then you are an artist. It's because you have to answer these questions now. You know the questions, because we are all in the same time, in the same moment. So all the questions you have in your head, these are the same questions I have. We are all in the same situation.

The question comes with the time. Different time, different question. *Leonardo Da Vinci*, he answered the time, so artists had to make science, to become scientists. Now it's 2015, and there are other questions.

Maybe interdisciplinary. And I will say, to make people a bit slower. Take this dance, don't make it so quick. Think about what you do. Look around, there is art everywhere. You don't have to go to a museum. You don't have to go to a gallery. Just open your fucking eyes, there is art everywhere. That's it. That's the question now, I guess.

For example, I know about this

in China. Over the past 15 years, maybe 20 years, there were maybe 10 museums in China. And now after 20 years, there are maybe 2,000 of them. Every day they open a museum somewhere in China. And it's good, I would not say it's bad. I just think about art – and girls.

Did you ever think about, if not being an artist, what other job you would do?

None. (Pause) Oh, I also want to be an archeologist. But I chose to be an artist.

www.vimeo.com/diridollou

Francois，32岁，现居柏林（来自法国）

2015年8月3日
采访于柏林Prinzessine花园

你可以自我介绍一下吗？

我叫Francois。我来自法国的布列塔尼区，那是法国非常好的一个区域。在我来柏林之前，我在那里学习艺术。后来我开始到德国进行了很多次交换生的学习。我本科在好几个不同的地方学习了艺术史，文化和文化科学。我在巴黎国立美院学习了四年并拿到了学位。后来，我到柏林来念硕士。但是我没有上完，因为课程内容太无聊了。我那时脑子里想着很多事情，所以不得不停下来重新考虑一下我的人生。

你来柏林多久了？

我一直在柏林断断续续地居住。如果把所有的时间都加在一起，那至少有三年了。最近的这次我已经在这呆了一年。不过我很快又会回法国。我可不想再在这里过另一个冬天。不想。

你回法国干嘛？

还没确定。我会在老家和巴黎两地往返。今年九月我的一个艺术家朋友邀请我去巴黎做一个艺术项目。然后十月份我在斯特拉斯堡又有另一个项目。

我很讨厌“项目”这个词。但是有时候我不得不用它。我是那种不愿意谈论项目的艺术家。我也不想申请什么东西。我有时候会尝试申请一下，因为我不知道要怎样才能进入艺术圈。但是我又不想进去。所以这是个问题。

为什么不想进艺术圈？

因为我不喜欢他们做事的方式。我喜欢艺术，我创作艺术，我想要展览。但是我不喜欢艺术圈的游戏，我也不想参与那游戏。

所以你做什么样的艺术？

我做录像装置。我的学位就是主攻这个方向的。那是我的研究。创作的起点是工作中的艺术家，一个用自己的身体来连接艺术的艺术家。在我还不是艺术家，而只是一个学习艺术史的学生的时候我就已经做了很多研究。

你对艺术家的定义是什么？

我没有一个定义。我想应该是自由的人想要带给人们一些东西，并且真的有兴趣做些能改变世界的富有创意的事吧。我们有各种不同的武器。但是如果你想要成为艺术家，你就需要决定是否运用艺术的武器。

打个比方，当我在做录像的时候，我想要用现代的工具，所以我没有选择画画。我想要用我的敌人－大众传媒所使用的工具。因为如果我要针对它说些什么，我就必须要用和它一样的媒介语言。

我也不是个电脑高手。我小时候都没有看过电视。一直到22岁我才有了人生第一台电脑。所以我需要学习所有的技术。不过我习惯图像并知道如何分析它们。

首先，我知道如何去分析一个图像。然后，我再做录像来对这张图像说点什么。我很少采用摄像机的运动。我只有我的身体和一台三脚架，没有团队。像一个画家一样，只是我用摄像机作画。

你有作品集网站吗？

我真的不喜欢这些网络的东西。不过我有Vimeo

账户，它和Youtube有点像，但是某种程度上要更专业些，而且更具保护性，尊重你所做的东西。

你为什么不喜欢网络？

我喜欢网络可以用来保持联络的功能，那部分挺好的。网络对我来说是关于连接。如果你想要上网找些什么，为什么不呢？但是如果要展示什么东西，我真的不觉得那是最好的方式。

当我在网上看电影的时候，总是会存在另一个可能性。这个可能性就是我可以和现实有更多连接。所以我选择那另一个选项。我可以读一本书，去看一场电影。我遇见一个女孩而不是上色情网站。事实上，那样要好多了。我试着做在现实中的事。要不然，你就会迷失在网络无尽的可能性中。

人们在网络上展示的东西，它们也在现实中的某处存在。所以我宁愿去它们在现实中展示的地方。去遇见新的人，在眼神的对视中交换讯息。

柏林的生活怎么样？

这里真的很舒服，也很大。没有很多人，但是空间非常宽阔。我现在住在Wedding区。这是一个正在新兴的时髦区域。

我总是住在新兴的区域。我第一次来柏林的时候，那是八到十年以前了。那时我住在Prenzlauer Berg区，那时候已经是美好时光的尽头了。然后就开始了士绅化进程。

士绅化是一个渐进的过程。并且现在它正在Mobbit区发生。而我是其中的一部分。艺术家们是士绅化的中心。他们发现新的地方，然后在那里开一个小酒吧或是其他小而美好的东西。然后他邀请他的朋友们也过来。接着投资方面的人就跟来了，生意人，房地产商，都过来赚钱。然后他们就把那块地方变得越来越贵，并逐渐把人们赶走。

你觉得柏林有太多艺术家了吗？

我不在乎。我真的不在乎。

真的吗？那你觉得周围有这样一个艺术家的社群更好吗？

这都是很偶然的。我的朋友们全都是艺术家。他们中的大多数都和艺术有关系或是从事艺术。我的生活就是这样。这是很正常的事。我遇到和我一样对生活有相似看法的人。但我对艺术圈不感兴趣。我不去画廊，也不常去美术馆。我以前上学的时候还挺常去的，因为那时学习就是我的工作。但是现在，这些都结束了。

所以你就只是做你自己的事？你也不在乎所谓的艺术世界在发生什么？

我真的不在乎。我看得很清楚。我不需要出去也知道在发生什么。我是个很聪明的人。我不需要到处参加活动才能理解在发生什么。因为我一直都在学习那些东西。我知道所有的小技巧。我也一直在工作。我尝试寻找并和那些跟我做类似事情的艺术家和社群保持联系。我们不会做流行的东西，而是做跨界的尝试。我做了个木工房并声称那其实是艺术。

对你来说，做艺术家或是做艺术其实是一种生活方式吗？而不是变得职业化以寻求在画廊或美术馆的艺术世界里发展？

如果有美术馆或画廊邀请我也不错啊。我肯定会答应的。

但是你有在往那个方向努力吗？你有在尝试吗？

我努力做自己并保持自我。我不想为了他们能接受我而去做些什么。我不要去想他们想要什么。因为如果我开始这样做的话，我就会迷失自己。我会丢失了我的创造力。我会丢了我的艺术。就算我还能拥有那些，但是，去他的。我可不想要他们。

艺术家对他们来说只是工具。"他们"是指美术馆，画廊和策展人。他们把自己的名字放得比艺术家还大。他们说他们组织了什么。他们打造了艺术家的梦之队。然后他们就掌控了一切。而我们就只不过是他们为了达到目的而需要的道具。这样他们就可以获得很多认可和金钱。

比如，他们就不会选我。因为他们知道我会批评他们。所以他们只会选那些愿意玩他们的游戏的艺术家。因为那类艺术家并不想要做艺术，他们只想要挣钱。他们想着，为什么不做艺术家呢？人人都可以做艺术家啊。

我想要拥有世界。我也想要拥有自信和我的

乐趣。总之，可能我就是不在乎吧。可能我会在两百年以后才会为世人所知。如果我所做的对世界有好处，那挺好。如果没什么意思，那就没意思吧。

我更愿意从更宏大的角度考虑事情。所以，那些小小的画廊世界，小小的当代艺术，那些小把戏，我尽量远离。但是我知道方向。因为我学的就是这些。所以我不回答我自己的问题，而是回答艺术史和时代的问题。现在我们到达了一个阶段，有一些问题需要被回答。所以有一些艺术家就需要去回答这些问题，现在就要。

比如哪些问题？

跨学科，跨媒介。把各种不同的艺术和人交融在一起。让人们知道这比仅仅做一件艺术品或仅仅做一名艺术家要更复杂。

并不是说你做了一件艺术品你就是艺术家。而是因为你需要现在就去回答这些问题。你知道这些问题是什么，因为我们都生活在同样的时代、同样的时刻。所以你脑子里有的所有问题也是我脑子里会有的问题。我们都是一样的。

问题总是随着时代而来的。不同的时代会有

不同的问题。列奥纳多·达·芬奇回答了他的时代，所以那时候艺术家也需要是科学家。现在是2015年了，我们还有其他的问题，也许是跨学科。以及让人们慢下来。跳支舞，不要那么快。思考一下你做的事。看一看周围。你不一定要去美术馆，你也不需要去画廊。你只要睁开你的眼睛。艺术无处不在。就是这样。这就是现在的问题。

比如，我知道中国现在的情况是，在过去15到20年里，整个国家都只有大概十家美术馆。但是现在，20年以后，可能已经有两千家。每天都有一个新的美术馆在中国某处开张。这是好事，我不会说这是坏事。我就是只想着艺术。还有姑娘们。

你有想过如果不做艺术家，你会做什么别的工作吗？

没有。哦，我也想当个人类学家。但是我选择了艺术。

www.vimeo.com/diridollou

Lehua, 28 years old, Shangha

Interviewed in Shanghai
September 11th, 2013

Please introduce yourself.

My name is Lehua Zhang, I'm a young artist living in Shanghai.

How old are you?

28, I'm a cancer.

What kind of works do you do?

Recently, I've been doing a lot of painting, and video works. But to be honest, I don't have a clear definition of what kind of work I do. It's a mixture of things. Maybe my recent energy is good for painting and video. It's easier to do these types of works, easier to realize them. So that's what I've been doing recently. I used to do live performance or installations, but not in the last two or three years.

What are the subjects of your work?

My works are usually the products of the mixed states of one's personal life in the context of art and society. It's a bit vague. I can't deliver a speech like some other artists saying my work is about science, or this and that. But I can naturally mix the information that I perceive in my personal life, then have a dialogue with the current happenings in the art world. Basically, it's within the context of modern and contemporary art, but at the same time drifting apart from the specific context… ehhh, I'm afraid it's too vague, I don't even know what am I talking about now.

Are you Shanghainese?

Yeah.

As a Shanghainese artist living and working in Shanghai, can you tell us more about the state of the art world in Shanghai as you know it?

Generally, there are Beijing and Shanghai as the two main cities for art in China. But when looking at art resources, Shanghai is not at the same level as Beijing. Shanghai is like a tourist city, although Shanghai may have the most art museums in China now. Just last year, there were quite a few private museums opened in town. You know, it's just a bunch of rich people. They had their business corporation first, then they build the museums. They collected a lot classical contemporary art. Hmmm, many big events have happened in Shanghai, maybe about the same as Beijing.

But lets talk about the living standard of artists in Shanghai. It's much looser in Shanghai. Or you can say the galleries in Shanghai are not at the same level as those in Beijing. A lot of foreign galleries still prefer to go to Beijing and thus build it as a cultural center. And then many artists follow and move to Beijing, for example the Black Bridge art village around 798, etc.

It's different than the situation in Shanghai. You might think there is a group of artists in Taopu, or a group that's always surrounding ShanghArt gallery. But they are still minorities. It's a really really small group. And the rest of the young artists would even prefer to gather less as groups. There used to be some groups, but not anymore. This is my objective observation. Artists here are not as career-minded and motivated as artists in Beijing. They live a more casual life, and have less pressure for exhibitions than Beijing artists. Artists in Beijing are more ambitious. They want to stand out. But artists in Shanghai are much more gentle on that.

What has changed in the art circle in Shanghai in recent years?

I don't think there has been substantial change. Artists progress really slowly. They do exhibitions one after another. Some young artists would come out, and some others would disappear when they can no longer handle it. Just like that.

As for you personally, what changes have you had after your graduation?

When I first graduated, I told myself, I should survive first. So I decided to work as a teacher. I was a high school art teacher, teaching art academy prep classes. It takes a bunch of my time, while at the same time I can't find the right state of mind to make my work.

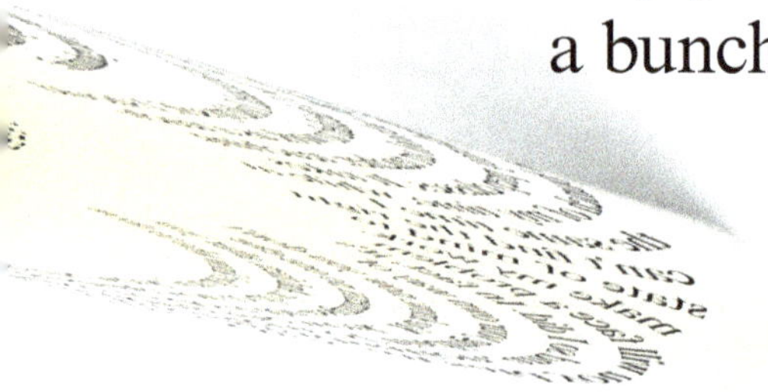

They all said you will face a problem after graduation, and so I did. In fact, it's a problem of finding your own way of making the work. You know, now you don't have to do it for assignments, no one else is pushing you to do it. And then, after you make the work, you don't know who to show it to. So now you really start to make works for yourself. There is no institution to tell you what to do. I didn't even have a gallery at the time. And the old ways of making works from back in school don't work anymore. There is no equipment support, there is no studio... So everything is like back to the very beginning, back to ground zero.

And the money you earn by working is gone very quickly after buying food and drink. So, I was relying on the energy I had left from recently graduating, making exhibitions with young artists in Shanghai. But after a while, things just can't keep on going anymore. Because the fundamental problem of creation still remains unsolved. You don't have a daily working routine. It's a quite annoying thing because that means you don't have a clear direction.

Then, in 2009, I had a solo exhibition in Beijing. Through some social networking, someone over there invited me to do an exhibition in an art space in Beijing. After that exhibition, I realized I had vomited all my big and small issues through the exhibition. I didn't care if people understood my work or not. I just had to put all my effort into it, slowly build up a complete solo show. That was my first solo exhibition. And I didn't sell any work from it.

After that, I kind of stopped for a while. I didn't make any work for over a year. I was just staying at home, sending away the last class of my students. Later, I did some projects with Doulebfly (an artist collective), went to Switzerland, and some other stuff. Many times I had no money to live during the year…yeah.

So then, I set a goal for myself. I had to try to see if I could support myself solely by selling artworks, whether it would be selling paintings or something else. So, it was from then that I started to think that at least paintings sell. A graphic work is still easier to sell. What I used to not be willing to do, maybe now I can try to do it and at the same time not make myself look too bad. So I did. And I started working with galleries. And then one thing just led to another.

Did you sell?

Yeah, but for very little money, just a few thousand RMB, but at least it's selling, someone is buying it. My painting is not bad, right?

So do you now have a better idea of how to work as a professional artist?

Yeah, I'm still learning. Because we all know that it's something we didn't learn at school. They never taught us how to become a professional artist. They taught us how to create, how to make a project proposal, or how to look like an artist. But we never learned how to become a real professional artist.

Or maybe, the teachers didn't know themselves. Because they were living in a different time period when they started to make art works. But our generation, living in such a peaceful environment, we can't make things happen by just holding on and struggling. We need professional training and skills. And it takes time to learn. So we can only try to figure it out slowly.

In fact, I like to be forced to figure things out. All my learning experience, I learned by slowly figuring it out myself. I'm quite a slow and stubborn person. Some problems other people may have realized from the very beginning, but I never did. Even now, I don't think I'm clear on some things. I may rather spend time wondering about shallow questions like 'What is art?'

How do you look at the necessity of making art works in the context of the current state of Chinese social society? Or in other words, the relationship between art and society in China?

There are two questions in your question. One is a very big question, which is 'What's the function of art?' I think we have to first realize, no matter what happens with the living standard of the artist, whether he's poor or rich, that's a financial problem. But with art itself, in the end, those that are written into art history, it's rather a question of whether it had any influence on people, whether it updated peoples' aesthetics. Or, from a sociological point of view, whether art has reminded people about the loss or chaos of society, the alienation of human beings. That's what art and artists should do. And history has proven that's what they have been always doing, and that's what they are supposed to do.

And the so-called 'avant-garde' is referring to a status of being ahead of time. Art should be ahead of its time. If it's not avant-garde, it's not carrying out the function we just talked about. Because if it's ahead of its time, it makes people confused, or refreshes their way of thinking. So it can push society forward from an aesthetic point of view. So it can remind people, hey, we have been following the mainstream culture for a long time, and now we realize there is actually a problem. Look at where we are now. That makes us think about the problem from another perspective. And that's better. It's a sacrifice that artists make. They provide another value system to let others understand. That's what art and artist should do.

Then comes the problem of China's relationship with the western world. Chinese contemporary art has a special fucking problem, that is – China has no culture itself. I'm talking about the recent history of China. There is really no culture. So what are we going to do? Of course we copy from the west. It's the same as any other industry in China. They all copy from the west. Some other people may be even more direct. Take for example, the design industry, it's fucking direct copying, and making it their own. But it works. It may look indecent. But even a gangster can be someone significant once he dresses up well. Once he has the money, he can dress up like a gentleman. A long time ago, when the west was quite poor and in chaos, they were looking for solutions from the east to renew themselves too. That's what we call 'the turning of Fengshui'.

What is your life like right now? How are you balancing your art and life?

I'm still trying to support myself by selling my work. I have to do this. So I'll really put my effort into it.

Because our understanding of art, from undergrad to now, has already been framed, such as how we position ourselves, what we do, what we don't do. So the rest of it, let's be vulgar, let's say we are aiming for money, and then there is no longer a problem.

Because sometimes, money can be a driving force. Sometimes we have misunderstandings that we say some artists are making art for money, making paintings for the living room. But I think if you are still not thinking about the money problem at this point, and only thinking about how great or noble you are, then you are really making a mistake. You will make your life miserable. In the end, you are not making art. Instead, art is fooling you. I'd rather say hey, I need to make some money, so let's make some work. Make some paintings. So when you are making the painting you are aiming for money, but during the process, you are still in the broader framing just like I said before, you are still doing something fun, that's enough.

Do you have a 3–5 year plan? What's your plan for the coming years?

Yeah, I need a 3–5 year plan. I need to start working with bigger organizations. I can continue with my current status in Shanghai for at most 1–2 years. I can't be satisfied with these…I mean, they can financially support me at the moment. But this can't be my goal. It can't be, because the scene is too small, and ShanghArt gallery is full now. There is only one bigger institution in Shanghai, really, only one, because museums don't have direct interaction with artists.

So, I will probably go to Beijing. I have to start looking and start building relationships with them. I'm not sure if I really have to go live there. It depends on my financial situation and other factors. I think it's possible to go live there, if finances permit. After all, moving is a big expense. At least for now, I can't afford a big move in my life. I will only go if I can confirm I'm going to get the resources I want, and that they need me to be there. Otherwise, I don't think it's necessary. But really, there are a lot of resources over there. If you want to make art works in China, and you don't have connections with organizations in Beijing, no one will see your work. It's always the same people in Shanghai, not to mention if you want to be international.

What about other young artists in Shanghai? Do you communicate with them?

You want to ask about those who are doing better?

How do you define what's better? Are you

talking about those who have representation?

In the younger generation like us, it's hard to not mention artists like *Lu Yang*, who is really ferocious, always very high and energetic, going abroad to make projects, and having interdisciplinary cooperation with other institutions. To me, she is a very good practitioner. For example, she is really working with comic, medical, and scientific disciplines. She is making the effort to do it. Although in the end, it's still just an image, because you can't escape the frame of visual art. But it's really a very good gimmick, because you are now really doing new media artwork. You are indeed interdisciplinary now. Then you have established your identity.

You were doing some exchange projects with overseas organizations, and many young artists go abroad to do artist residency programs nowadays. How do

you see these things?

I can't handle it. Of course I want it. I want to do artist residencies. I want to have a reason to go to Europe. Because it's really lame to go there just for the sake of visiting my girlfriend. Then I'm only a tourist. Granted I can visit museums, which is nutritious. I have been to Spain twice, the only thing I can do is go visit museums. But it's not a plan for the long term. I need to get into an artist lifestyle over there, make some work. I need an artist residency. I applied, but couldn't get one. Europe is in a financial crisis now, and a lot of financial support is gone. They'd rather you give them some money to do the residency. That's doesn't suit me.

In 2016, **Lehua Zhang** is still working as an artist, and he is starting to accept being called a 'painter'. He jumps between different series of works in search of greater and simpler threads of creation.

He is now the father of a one-year-old boy, traveling between family housework and the art studio. He has two studios in Shanghai: one big, one small – one is far away, and the other is nearby home. He uses them alternately every other day.

He keeps his exhibition frequency at the pace of two solo shows a year, plus several other group shows. His work has been shown in Shanghai, Hong Kong and Paris.

乐华，28岁，上海

2013年9月11日
采访于上海

先介绍一下你自己？

我的名字叫张乐华，我是生活在上海的一个年轻艺术家。

多大年纪了？

28。巨蟹座。

你具体做什么样的艺术作品？

最近，最近画画呀。也做录像嘛。但其实的话，我没有对自己有明确界定是做什么东西。就做一些混来混去的东西吧。就是对媒介已经没有特别明确的划分了。我已经特别模糊了。最近的能力可能比较适合画画和录像。比较方便地来做，也比较容易实现，那我最近就做这个。以前也做现场和装置类的东西，但最近的两三年里面没有做过了。

你的作品一般是关于什么样的主题？

我的作品，一般都是在个人的生活和艺术以及社会的这么一个交错的状态里面产生的吧。比较模糊。我不能像某些艺术家直接说出来我关心什么东西，是科学啊，或者是什么的。但我会比较自然地在自己的生活的经历上面，把我能看到和听到的信息混杂起来，然后和艺术的现状来产生一个关系吧。然后这基本上还是基于一个现当代艺术的语境里面。但是又稍微地有点疏离于这个很确切的语境。啊，说得太模糊了。都不知道自己在干嘛。

你是上海人？

我是。

你能介绍一下作为一个生活在上海的艺术家，你所了解的上海艺术圈是怎样的一个状态？

普遍来讲，因为有北京和上海两个点嘛。但是其实从艺术资源来讲，上海和北京还不是一个档次的。上海更加像一个旅游城市。现在有美术馆最多的城市估计就是上海了。在去年都开了好几个私立的私营美术馆。就是一些有钱人，他们建立的集团，然后有美术馆。他们收藏了大量的经典的当代艺术的东西啊什么的。嗯，有很多大事儿在上海发生，有可能跟北京不相上下。

但是从艺术家本身的生存来讲呢，上海更松散。或者说画廊行业更“低档”，就是说水准不够。大量的国外的画廊资源还是到北京去，把他们建立成了一个文化中心。所以随之而来的就是大量的艺术家也生存在北京。像798周围的黑桥艺术村一类的。

上海呢，情况又不一样。上海听起来好像有桃浦，好像总有一群艺术家，围绕在香格纳画廊身边的一群艺术家，总是在聚在一起。但其实也是非常的小众，非常非常地小众。其他的年轻艺术家就更加地不抱团了。以前也有曾抱过团，但不管从艺术家的性格来讲，还是从艺术家的生存方式来讲，都不成气候。对，这也是我很客观的判断。艺术家的生活状况是松松散散的。对于展览本身的诉求也并没有像北京的艺术家那样有压力，北京的艺术家非常渴求地在做事，他们期望自己会出来。但是上海呢，更绵软一点。

上海的艺术圈和几年前比起来有什么变化吗？

没本质上的变化吧。艺术家的进步很慢的嘛。都是在一个接一个做展览啊。有新的年轻艺术家冒出来，也有混不下去的年轻艺术家消失掉。恩，就是这样。

作为你个人来讲，从毕业到现在的这几年，是怎样的一个变化？

刚毕业的时候么，用一个做老师的借口，就是先生活下来咯，决定要做老师。大部分的重心也是要去做一个老师。做老师也要花时间的。一个高中的美术教师嘛。就是教考前班，一样的。但是听起来的话，时间也是占去了大部分。然后自己做作品的状态又完全不在嘛。

那大家都说毕业之后会遇到一个问题的，那我也是随之而来就遇到了那个问题。其实就是毕业之后，你开始自己创作的一个寻找过程。就是，你也不为作业做了，也没人推动你做了，然后你做了之后给谁看你也不知道。那还是要做，为自己做。也没有机构来管你。就是也没有什么画廊。当时也没有。然后在学校那种做法呢，比如说做现场什么的那种做法也不合适了。因为首先没有什么设备支持了。自己也没有工作室。回到上海之后基本上就像白手起家一样，就又回到高中时代嘛。

工作那点钱呢，买吃的喝的就完了。反正，当时借着毕业时候的那鼓劲儿嘛，还是可以做展览的。跟上海的年轻人一起做展览啊什么的。但是做着做着就软掉了。就是说创作本身的问题还是没有解决嘛。自己没有平时的工作状态嘛。没有一个日常的工作状态是一个很讨厌的事情。也就是方向不明确。

那后来一直到我09年在北京，因为08年毕业之后当时在北京有一些人际关系，所以就有人约了我一个个展。在北京的一个艺术空间。做了那个展览之后就发现，基本上就把自己的各种大大小小的状态啊，就呕吐掉了，在那个展览里面。也不管别人看得懂看不懂，反正就使劲做。磨磨蹭蹭地把一个个展拼出来，在没有任何个展经验的情况下面。反正我当时也没有任何买卖。就是这样的一个展览，就弄过去了吧。

然后那之后我就停掉了。我就有一年多都没有做作品。就是呆在家里面，把学生带完。最后一年的学生带完。然后后来也做了一些跟双飞有关的项目。去了瑞士啊，哪里啊……在忙那些项目。一年里面也经常断粮。恩，就是这种情况。但是就混过来了一年。

然后在那个之后呢，给自己的一个目标就是，无论如何要先用艺术这个事情看看能不能养活自己。不管是卖画还是什么的。所以呢，那个时候开始，那比较简单的想法是画画可以卖嘛。一个平面的东西还是容易卖。而且我也相信就是说，那些以前不太愿意做的事情，现在如果去做的话，我是可以把它做得并不让自己丢脸，但是又让它卖掉的。所以我就做了，也跟画廊合作了。一些事情就来了嘛。

卖了吗？

也卖了啊，就是非常少的钱啊。非常少的钱。几千块钱也可以卖掉，对伐。会有人买的。而且本来画得也不赖嘛，对吧。

现在你会不会比较有一个概念，就是怎么去做一个职业艺术家？

对，我在学习怎么去做一个职业艺术家。因为我很清楚，其实有些事儿在学校里面我们并没有学到。并没有教我们怎么去做一个职业艺术家。学校的老师教我们怎么创作，怎么想方案，或者说怎么有一个艺术家的范儿，对吧。但是我们并没有学到怎么样真正地去做职业艺术家。

或者有可能，他们自己都不明白。因为他们自己在那个年龄和时代做艺术，状况不一样嘛。那我们现在在这么和平的一个情况下，不是说靠一股劲儿就能把事情给憋出来的。还是要靠一些职业素养和技巧的。要去学的。那只能靠自己慢慢摸咯。

而且我也是被逼地喜欢摸。所有的学习过程都是自己慢慢摸出来的。很笨，很慢的一个人。也许很多人刚毕业他就已经把很多职业的东西都已经学会了。为什么做艺术，怎么做，这些问题有些人一开始就懂。但是我也完全不懂，到现在也可能想地都没有别人明白。可能，我也更愿意把心思总是花在“艺术到底是什么”这样肤浅的问题上。

你怎么看所谓在中国现在社会状况之下做艺术的必要性？或者说在中国，艺术和整个社会状态之间的关系？

你刚才这个问题里面是两个问题，一个是大了去了的问题，就是艺术到底是干嘛用的。那这个我觉得，我们首先要看清楚，艺术家怎么着，这是艺术家自己生存状态的问题。他穷死了或者富死了，那是经济上的事儿。那艺术本身，到后来，到最后，就是说被归纳到美术史之后，那其实看的是它在当时有没有影响到人们，更新了人们的审美。或者说在社会学上来说，它是不是对社会所谓的这种失去的状况，或是社会的混乱，还有人的异化，有没有起到提醒，让人保持清醒的一种作用。这个是艺术和艺术家应该做的份内的事儿。而且事实证明就是，一直以来他们都在做这个事情。他们应该做。

而且所谓的前卫的意思就是说，它是一个前卫的状态，其实艺术它应该是前卫的。艺术不前卫，它就起不到我刚刚说的那个作用。因为它前卫了，所以让人产生了困惑或者是思维上的刷新。那它才起到了从美学上的一个点去推动社会进步的状况。或者说提醒人们，“啊，我们其实是跟着所谓的主流文化跟了很长时间才发现它有问题。或者是我自己的生存状态已经成这样了，我才看到一个另一面去考虑这个问题。”那这样比较好一点，这是艺术家拿自己做的一个牺牲。然后提供出的一个价值观，让你来看到。那这样还不错。这个是艺术和艺术家应该做的事情，就是我们怎么去看它。

然后就是又牵扯到中国和西方的这个事儿。那是当代艺术本身特有的一个很操蛋的问题。就是因为中国本身，它没有文化。我是说近代中国啊，没有文化。这是真的没有文化。那怎么办?呢那当然就是从西方弄过来了。这是全部的中国艺术，和中国的任何产业在做的事情是一样的呀，都是从国外搬过来。有些人做得更直接。你去设计行业看，他妈的不是更直接嘛。直接去抄东西过来，然后把它变成一个东西。但是这一步也是有效的呀。就是这种拷贝看起来有点下流，有点流氓。那流氓到后来，他打扮好了，他也是一牛逼人物呀，就是等他有钱以后，他也可以把自己装扮成一个斯文人的。包括以前，你说当西方很破乱的时候，他们不是也在寻求东方的东西在更替自己吗？风水轮流转呀。

你现在的生活状态是怎样的？你是怎样在平衡你的创作和生活这两部分？

我还是尽量让自己的创作可以养活自己吧。我需要去这样去做。那好好做的话，就是……那好好做就是……我操，“好好做”太操蛋了。就是认认真真做吧。

因为就是我们自己对艺术的理解，从大学一直到现在。定位啊，受谁的影响，怎样定位这个事儿，大框架已经定了。我们做什么东西，不做什么东西，已经基本上给自己预设了。那然后剩下的事儿啊，我们粗俗一点，就冲着钱去，问题就不大了。

因为有时候，钱，它必须是一个动力。有时候对伐，就是有时候我们的误会是什么呢，就是说有些人光为钱做艺术，画一张行画什么的。我觉得现在如果说在这个阶段，你要是还十分不想钱的话，搞的自己很牛逼很高尚呢，那就有点错了。就真的是把自己的生活给弄错了，你会把自己的生活弄得很惨。最终搞不定艺术这件事情。就被耍了嘛，被艺术耍了。那还不如我更纯粹一点。操，要去赚点钱吧。那就做点东西出来，画点东西出来。那画出来这个东西，目标是钱，但你这个过程当中做的东西还是跟以前那个大框架是统一的，你还是在做好玩的事情，那么就好了。

你有没有一个三到五年的计划？或者是后面一阶段准备怎么去安排的打算？

要的吧，三到五年的计划，我会。我要跟更大的机构合作啊。在上海一直保持在这个状态，能再保持一两年最多了。我不能再跟上海的这些……就现在他们也有养活我，但是这一定不是目标，就是说。不可以。因为局面太小了。然后香格纳又满仓了。大型的机构在上海只有一个。真的只有一个。其他的美术馆它不直接跟艺术家发生关系嘛。

所以还是要去北京吧，可能。要找，就是要跟他们建立联系。我不确定我是不是真的一定要去生活。这个也要看经济和各种问题。我觉得经济能够搞定的话，去那边生活也是有可能的。因为要搬迁是一笔大支出嘛。至少我现在的状况，还不够来一次大的变迁。就是要确定我可以得到资源我才会过去。而且得需要我过去才会过去。没必要，至少我现在觉得没什么必要。但是的确大量资源在那边。你在中国做艺术如果不跟北京的机构有什么关系的话，谁能看到你呢。老是看来看去就上海人的这些事儿，更别提你要国际化了。

那其他的年轻艺术家是怎么样的一个状态？你们有没有交流？

你是想问做得更好的？

做的更好的是什么？已经被代理的吗？

我们年轻人里面，口碑，或者说大家不会不提的就是陆扬这种，很凶猛的。然后一直很high，体力很充沛地去国外做项目啊，然后跟其他的这种跨媒介的合作啊。其实在我看来，她是非常好的一个实践者。就是她真的去跟比如说动漫，医疗，科技这种合作。她的确是在做。虽然说最后的成品还是一个图像。因为还是逃脱不了所谓视觉艺术的一个框架嘛。只不过，当然这样的噱头非常好。你的确是新媒介了，你的确跨了。你的确跨出了这一步，那你就有一个身份。

你之前也去过一些国外的交流项目，然后现在也有很多年轻的艺术家去国外做些驻留什么的，你怎么看这个事儿？

我搞不定这个事儿啊，我当然想要啊，当然想去驻留。我也想有一个事儿去欧洲嘛。因为我纯粹去看我女朋友就很傻逼嘛，就是一个旅游。大不了逛美术馆。当然也有营养啊。我去了两次西班牙，然后我能做的事情当然就是逛美术馆了。但是你说，这也不是长久之际啊。我需要打入到一个艺术的生活状态里面去。而且最好自己做点事情。需要驻留啊，对啊。但是我就是申请不到。最近欧洲的经济状况也不好。很多东西都没有了。他们最好你去捐一点钱去给他们做驻留。这不适合我。

张乐华，2016年，仍旧是艺术家，并开始不排斥被称呼为“画家”，跳跃在不同系列中寻求个人更大化更简化的创作线索。

一岁孩子的父亲，生活往返于家务和工作室之间，在上海拥有一大一小一远一近两间工作室隔天轮流使用。

展览频率保持在每年两个个展以及若干群展，近一年作品分别在上海、香港、巴黎展出。

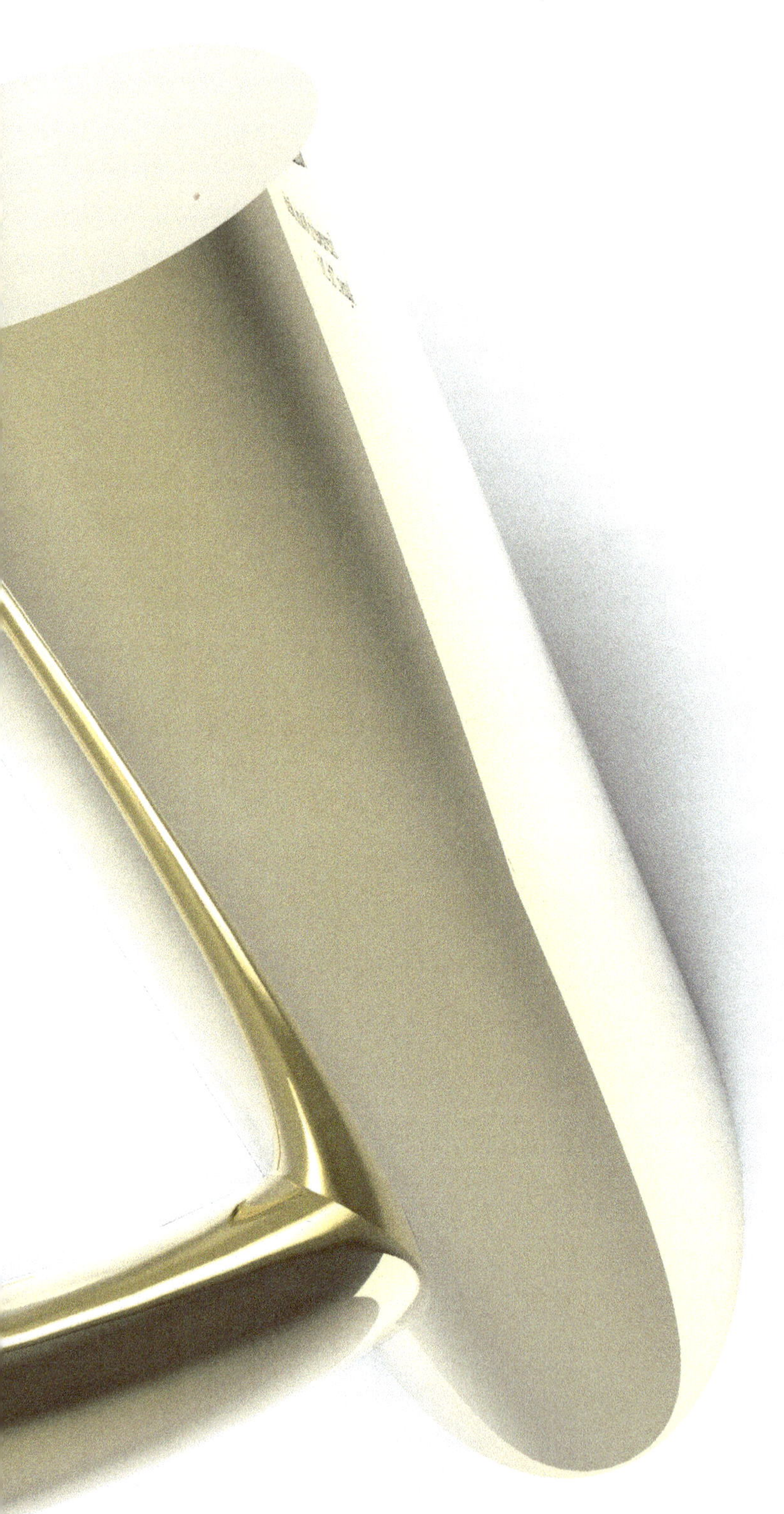

Matthias, 43 years old, Berlin

Interviewed in Moabit, Berlin
August 27th, 2015

So, I read something on your website about this place, but I also want to hear personal stories, the personal side of how you came to be doing this, and also maybe an introduction of how this place works. So, first, self-introduction.

I'm *Matthias*, and I'm one of the three directors of *ZK/U*, and I'm one of four members of the artist collective *KUNSTrePUBLIK*. There are overlaps. So the *KUNSTrePUBLIK* is the same as the *ZK/U* director board, except for one person who's living in Hamburg. And we've been running *ZK/U* for 3 years now, it was opened in August 2012. And before that, we've been working together for 8 years, so it has been quite a long time that we've worked together, almost more than 10 years.

We started off as an artist collective doing projects in public spaces. And through this journey of doing projects all over the world, and mostly also in Berlin of course, we realized we needed a stable base because in Berlin you have, as I guess all big cities, the problem of growing rents in the city ring. As artists we don't have incredibly high income, so we had to find a solution how we can stay in the city. So, we started to look for a building where we can sustainably stay and work, for ourselves. This was like 6 years ago. And then, we came across this building, and realized this cannot just be for ourselves, it's too big, we have to create something that is also for other people. And then we developed this concept of running a residency, for various reasons.

I will explain how *ZK/U* runs. *ZK/U* is basically divided in two parts. One is the public part; the other one is the private part. The private part is we have 14 residency spaces where artist from all around the world can work and live. They don't only work here, they also live here. And they stay between 2 months and 8 months. Our focus is on artists that are working in the urban arena that have questions towards how the city could look, how it's influenced by the city's past, how can influences from all over the world change a city. Yeah, so we are trying to gather together artists that are working in this field. Not only artists, but also people working scientifically in the field of research, like people coming from sociology. Architects, designers... and also people who are socially engaged. 'Cause our idea and focus is, as I mentioned, urban discourse.

But also, we are trying to bring together local community activities with activities from people coming from all over the world. Because this is something usually very difficult to bring together, I find. You know, very often you have residencies where artists do their stuff, and then they have an open house exhibit in galleries and so on. But there is no interaction between the actual environment of the residency and the residents. So this is something we want to focus on, and therefore, we have this second part of the building, the public space that we are sitting in now. This area plus the big hall, which is an exhibition hall, and then downstairs there is a cellar. These public spaces are for all kind of events.

We have open houses, we have an experimental flea market every two weeks, and we have every Friday experimental cinema, curated cinema with food, which corresponds to the films that are shown. And then, we have all kinds of workshops, seminars, and exhibitions of course. Different things that have the potential to attract people not only from the art scene or from the urban sciences, but also people that are just locals. And this is something we try very hard to realize, and it's not always easy. Because it creates some tension between sometimes the interest of the artists, or the interest of the broader public. The artists sometimes would rather just do their work and exhibit in galleries, and just want to stay

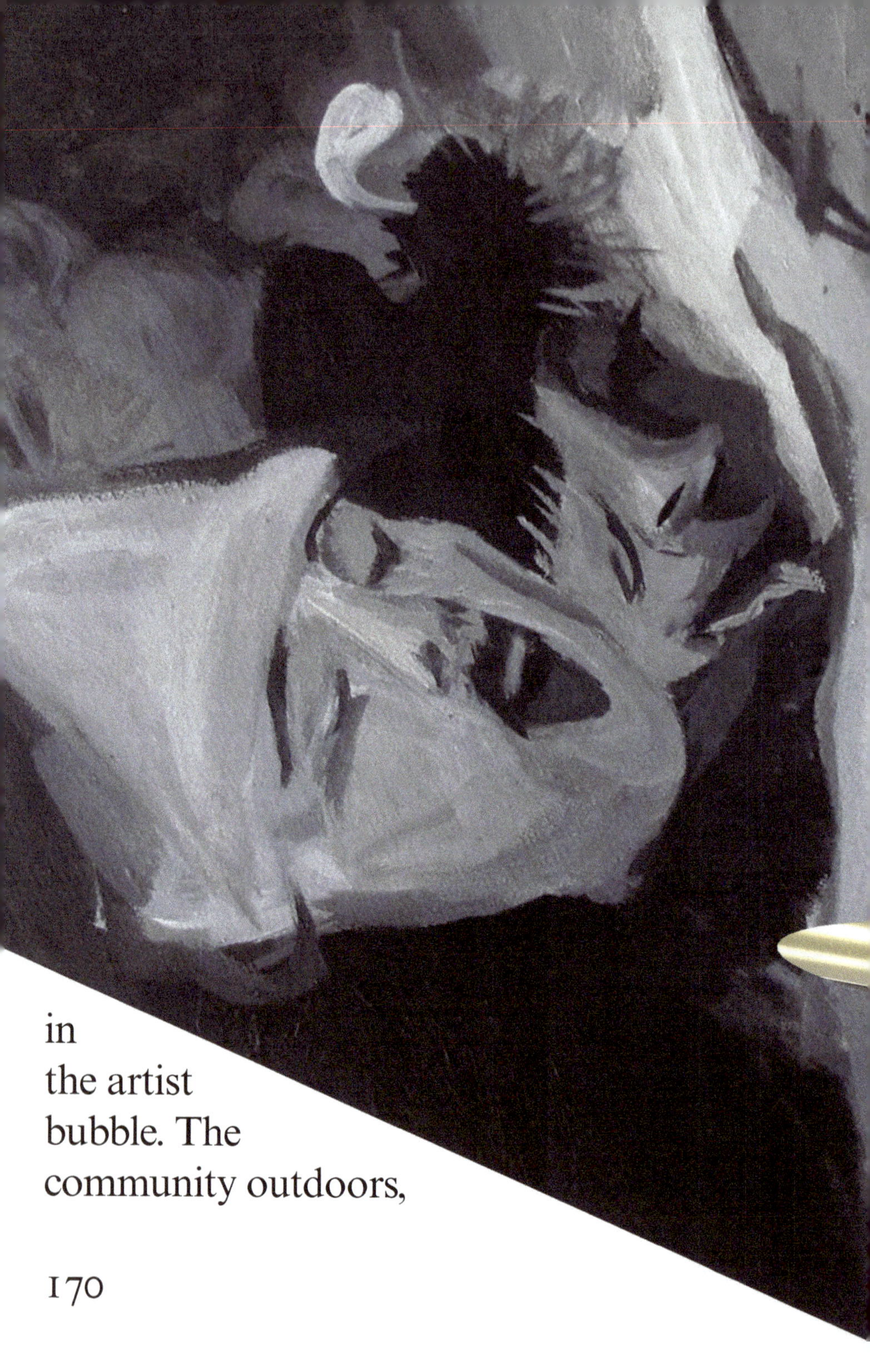

in
the artist
bubble. The
community outdoors,

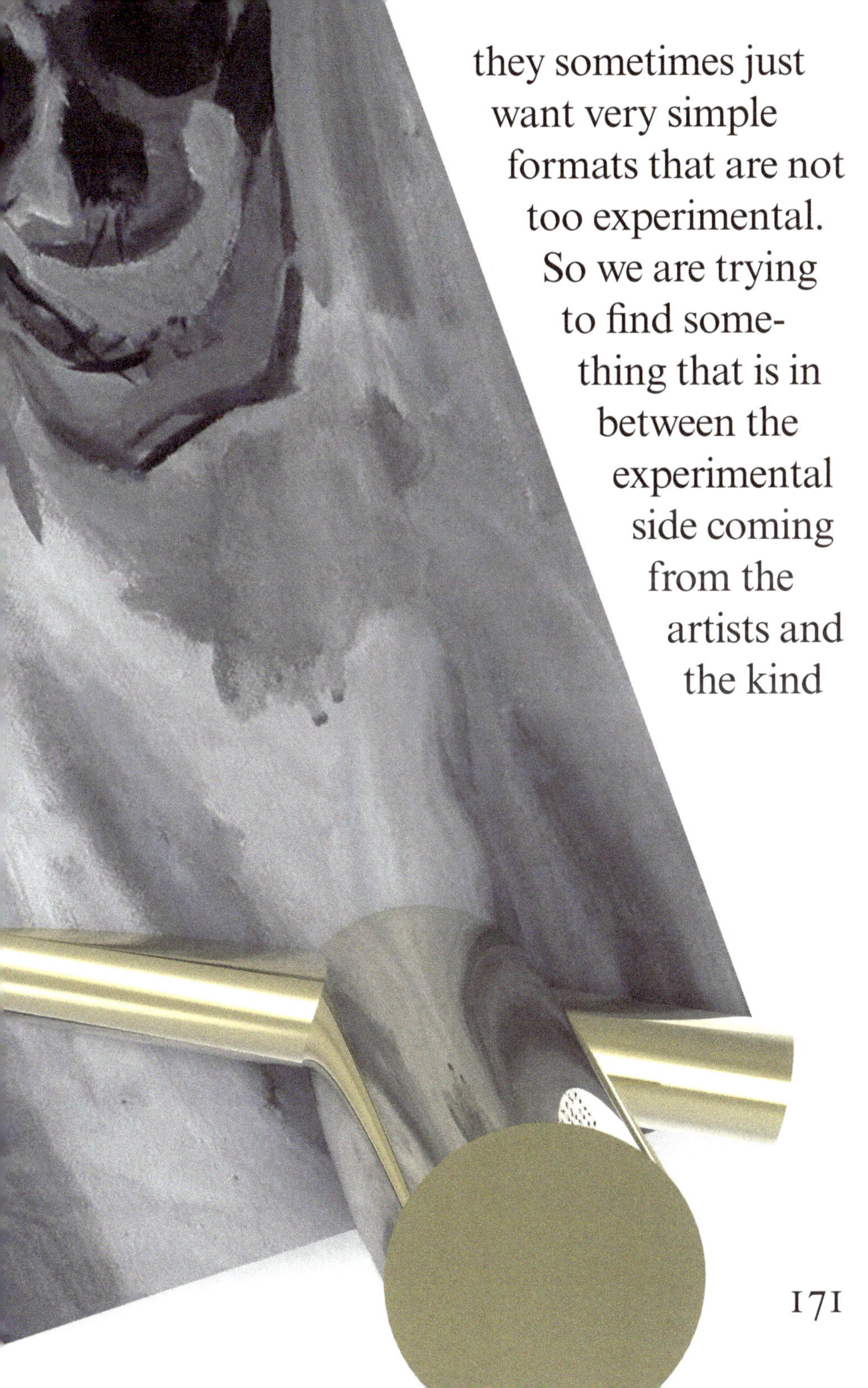

they sometimes just want very simple formats that are not too experimental. So we are trying to find some-thing that is in between the experimental side coming from the artists and the kind of attractive popular stuff, so people can actually come in and feel they are not totally in the wrong place. So this is kind of a tricky thing, but we think it's worth trying to build this bridge.

How did this intention grow and where did it came from? Does this have to do with the previous artist collective work you were doing?

Ah yes. Yes, exactly. We as an artist collective have always been interested in developing works which create some kind of social interaction. We work in public spaces mostly. We never really exhibit in galleries or museums and stuff. We do works that are very site-specific, they interact with local communities.

There is always a process that leads to the work, it's never like we come with an idea, and then we just build it, and that's it. It's always like, let's go to the place, we do research, we see what the parameters are, and then we develop works from these parameters. And two months later we do something that has something to do with the community where everyone works. So, that's the place where it's coming from. The idea that art is more than just form and message, but also process and social interaction.

It kind of connects to land art, or public art. But when you say you don't exhibit in galleries, is it because this is not the type of work that will sell at galleries, so they don't want to exhibit you? Or is it your statement of saying I actually don't to exhibit in galleries?

It's both. You know, it's really both. It's like on the one side, we don't create work that is sellable. I mean we create videos and photography stuff. But it's not attractive enough, on the other side, for the art market. I mean, maybe in the long run. But actually we are also not like 'No, we are not selling anything to anyone.' This is not like I don't care enough about the art market that I have such a strong negative or positive feeling about it. It's just not attractive for both sides. That's really it.

To me this is really interesting, because normally artists, when they want to make a career, they have to submit themselves into this art system in order to validate it and be recognized in this world.

Yeah, that's very tough work.

But it seems like you are now here with this space, and what you are doing here, creating your own system, it's a bit like an institution but not a real institution.

Yes, it's true. And there is never the intention to become an institution in that sense. Yeah, we do a lot of things, and it's becoming more like an institution, whether we like it or not. You know it's just naturally having a team now of 10 people, even more, 14 people. And having residencies for up to 20 people. You know it's really… so there are always around 14 people. You can organize it organically to a certain extent, but you have to start thinking about structures. Otherwise, you know… Things also repeat for us.

Artists come, they need to know what is the infrastructure, what can they do. Where do we go when we have this and that… You know, in the beginning of the time, it's also interesting to explain to people, but after a while… 'cause it repeats. And you also want to focus more on content. You know you want to focus more on curating stuff and developing ideas with the artists. So all these kind of infrastructural things you start to institutionalize it more. It's a natural development.

Nevertheless, our whole structure, we are three directors, I mean, this is a joke. We are three people, we funded this place, and we are trying to keep our hierarchies within the team really flat. No one wants to be the accounting idiot, and everyone would like to be only working artistically. So we have to share these kind of things.

But in 3 years, you've grown from only 3 of you guys to now a team of 10, plus artists. How did this happen? I mean, especially the financial part of it, how did you grow this? Where did the finance come from?

Sure, I can explain. So basically, we didn't have any cost in developing this place, because the development was funded. All the inside of the building is new, basically. So, this all got funded by different foundations. It was like we needed 1.6 million euros to refurnish the whole building. And we got the funding. So we don't have a bank loan to pay back, that put us in a good situation.

And then, basically, the residency works in two different ways. I mean, the residency creates the income, in the sense that we have contracts with the institutions that rent spaces and they then distribute to artists. So, you know, we have a partner in Korea who rents the place, it's an institution. And they send us a shortlist of artists that they think would fit in our space. And we make the final choice from the shortlist of who will come.

So this is one part, the other part is the open call that we have. Where we say, you apply, and if we like your work, we will send you all the papers necessary for you to find funding in your national or local structures that you come from. So a Canadian artist will get an invitation saying, 'We invite you for…' and they will tell us, 'Yeah, write research and exhibition.' So we write that.

And then, they can hand it to their local funding structures. And they have 3 years time after we've invited them to do this. Then, their stay is also funded, but by local structures in Canada. So these are the kind of two main tools.

And then also we have scholars that come, and they are doing a semester break, and they have a substantial income, so they just pay for the rent. And this income basically helps us to maintain the building and to help us run everything we run here, more or less. But it's not really enough, because the maintenance of the building is pretty costly. So we have to also create income through renting the place to other institutions that want to do exhibitions. But that's a tricky part, because you really have to see if it fits into your programing, is it too far out. You know, so we have to always look very closely. It's a curatorial question.

But right now it has been healthily balanced?

Yeah, more or less. I mean, you have your ups and downs, you know. I'm really happy with how the program has been developed. With the residencies, sometimes it's a bit tricky, because there are some difficulties. We work a lot towards residencies, like we have weekly joint dinners with presentations, we have curatorial visits, we offer them once a month to do an exhibition, and to have this open house. So they can decide whether they just want to do it in their studio, or if they really want to exhibit it.

But the more we offer, the more they need our personal attention, which is totally normal, of course. They don't know the infrastructure and so on. And this costs more money, because we pay people to do this. So the more you offer, the better you want to become, the more costly it becomes. And of course, also the more you have difficulties. You know, misunderstandings, etc. So it gets more complex. But this is where it starts getting interesting also.

As the director of this space, how is your day or week divided?

Yeah, that's also the tricky part. Since we still actually do quite a lot of art, and we still travel quite a lot. We got a project in Russia where we've been away for 4 weeks, so this is actually quite difficult. If we are not here, then things can really collapse, so we need to organize this really well. In a weekly routine, I'd say I'm working here four days a week. And I have one day and the weekend for doing my stuff, like artistic work, or just organizing my life. If you are working independently instead of employed by somebody, you have to spend a lot of time organizing your life without doing any art. So this is maybe another two days of the week, and maybe one day I'm not doing anything expect for hanging out at lakes.

But you also have 7 more employees, do you have to manage them? Do you have to tell them what to do? The programming part, and all the rest of running this space?

Yeah, yes we do. I mean we have kind of reccurring formats, so there are certain routines. So you don't have to tell people anymore, and they will manage. So our event coordinator, our residency coordinator, they know how to make contracts, how to communicate with the public and so on. But all the extra things, and there are quite a lot, we always have to sit together.

We have a weekly team meeting on Mondays, which is like 2–4 hours, quite long, but it's very important to inform each other about what's going on and where. And then, yeah, so we do have to sort of, to a certain extent, 'direct', but only to a certain extent. There is quite a lot of freedom for our employees to make decisions. On the financial side, I think we still need to keep the overview of course. And also, there is a certain stability of income, and how much people will get and so on.

Usually for artists, they just operate on their own, just one person. And then, I mean I guess you are used to working collectively with the group. And now it's really a big thing, a lot of things are happening, a lot of responsibility. It's also a very long-term commitment saying you are going to do this, make it happen…

Yeah yeah, that's also true. It's not fully resolved how much we like this. You know, I mean, we have a lot of fun here. And it's a great freedom we have, we can make so many decisions, it's amazing. But the administrative part is actually quite big. So I sometimes really wonder, hmm, I mean, do we still have enough time for doing artistic work? You know, this is of course a question. And so far, we've been lucky I would say. It's always been possible for us to do projects every year, a couple of projects. But in the long run, it's really stressful. We work very very hard to make these kind of artistic and administrative ends meet. You know, I wouldn't say, yeah, this is now and forever.

And I wouldn't mind maybe in a couple of years, maybe this has become so stable that we can slowly and smoothly kind of move out. Maybe I will be only serving on the advisory board, maybe just come here once a month. But now it's not the time, we still have to do so much funding work, basic work. I think it'll take another 5–10 years until this is really smooth.

But concerning your first question, we are totally used to working collectively. I mean I still work in two other collectives that I'm doing artistic work with. I'm also doing individual work, but I prefer working in a collective. It's more fun. I like this social interaction, all this is good, I like it. And you know, it helps you. You don't always have amazing ideas. There are times when you don't have great ideas, then you are stuck. And then there are people that inspire you in the collective. So this is really helpful. You don't get into this artistic crisis.

As an individual you can go into a really deep crisis. I mean, there were phases when I was only working individually, and I was really like, uhh, what am I doing, this is bad, my work is not good. And in a collective, it's more fun and you can relate to each other. But I think it's also healthier to think about how we as a collective are slowly moving out of this thing and letting a younger generation take it over, because for us as a collective we also have to change. And new challenges are really important. I think this is also what keeps us together. You know you have a new challenge. Ok, let's go for it. You know. It's bonding.

Is having and running this place also a statement for your artist collective?

Yeah, it is. We consider it as part of our artistic work. You know this kind of thing and how we develop it, the story was very tricky. I don't think any normal person would have gone through this process to build this thing, you know. No one, like an investor, would ever have done this. An architect would not have done this. No business-oriented person would have done this. So I think because it just didn't make sense, and it was too risky also. We took really a lot of risk when we started working on this thing.

This place was originally a train station?

Yes, it was a train station.

Does it belong to the government?

No longer, it belongs to us. I mean, we as the institution, the *KUNSTrePUBLIK* own the house. That's why it was so complicated. This is why we also put so much effort into this building. It's really a quite interesting construction. The land where the house stands belongs to the city government.

So the city government owns the land, we own the house. And this is part of the public park, so anyone could come in. So we have a lease for the land that this building stands on. And if the lease runs out, which is in 37 years, then the city government could say, we want our land back. This could happen in 37 years. If they want us to move somewhere else at that time, then they would have to pay the association *KUNSTrePUBLIK* money that the building has in value. So this is kind of a very lucky situation.

But on the other side, also I find it interesting because the local government does have some influence. In 37 years, they can say, ah it's no longer relevant. I find this is actually a good perspective for us, because in 37 years, both of us can have a decision again. I think this is good. Usually, land is sold to a private company or private owner, and the city can never influence it anymore, what's happening on this land. It's gone, forever. But in our case, we both can make decisions again.

And this kind of contract was very complicated. To develop this contract, and to find a base from the legal point of view was really complicated.

But 37 years is a really long time, what made you decide to commit yourself to this?

I mean we've always been doing projects where we didn't know what's going to happen in 2 years, or 1 year. But the reality of Berlin is that, if you don't find something more sustainable, you are gonna be kicked out, sooner or later, by the rent. As an artist, except if you become a really famous gallery artist, which is very unlikely.

The likeliness of it is very very low. So this is a reality that most of the students don't actually see. The chance of working in your job in Germany as an artist is like 2%. So you start going to art school, and 2% work out, and they will be working in the art field. Making a living by selling

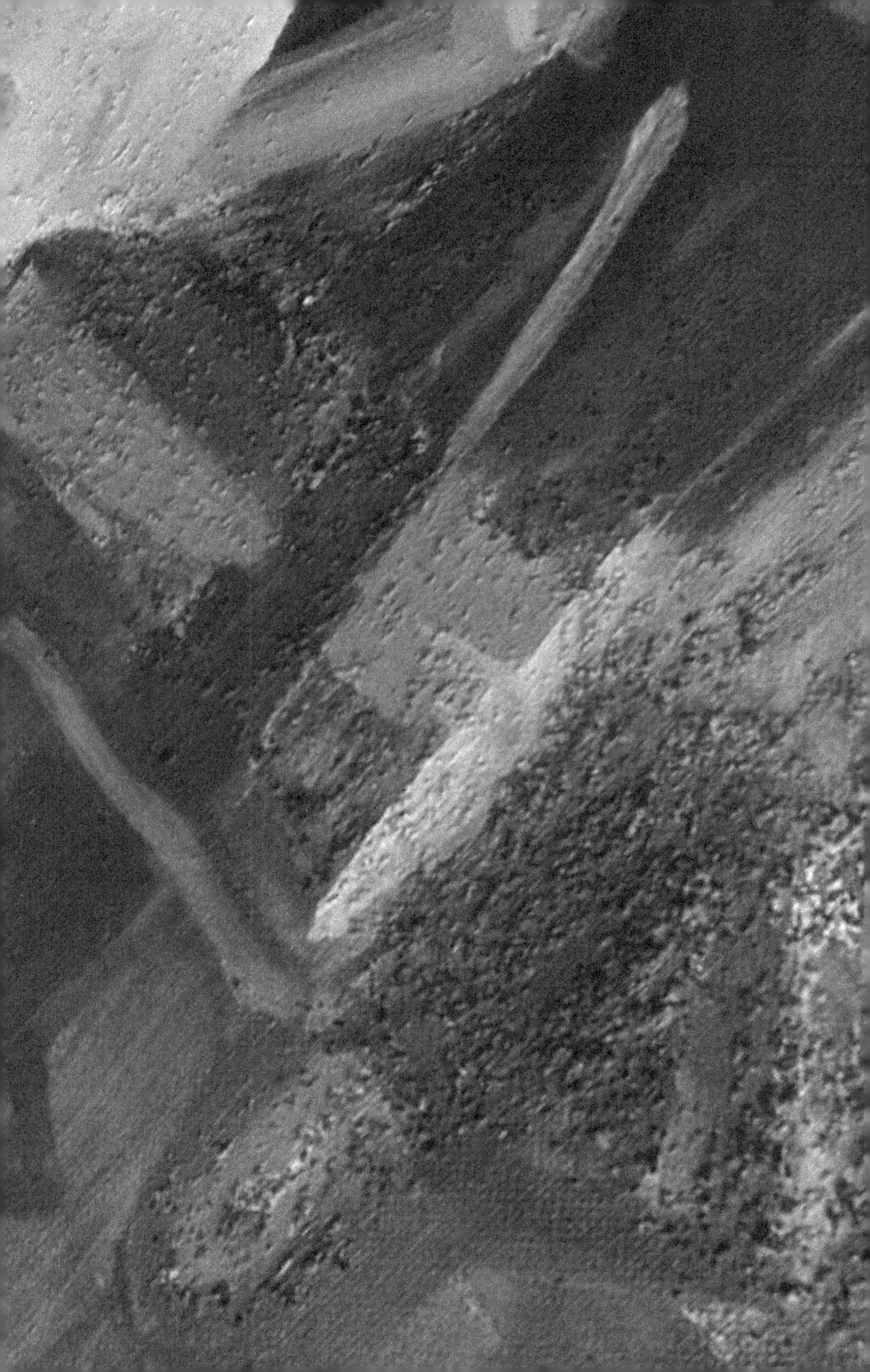

art or becoming maybe a curator is only 2%. All the other 98% they do something entirely different.

Or for a while, they get some funding, but at the same time they need another job.

Exactly. And then the other job will take over. (Laugh) This is how it is. The statistic is like they look at art students ten years after they finish their studies. Yeah, so this is the reality, the painful reality. So we also realize, hey, we've got to find a more sustainable model. Doing projects here, doing projects there, sooner or later we'll have to stop and do some odd jobs, or become teachers.

You might still be working somehow with what you've learned. But you will just do a different job. So we realize of course the special situation of Berlin is very complicated and getting more difficult. That's why we pushed for finding a place that's going to be there for longer. And it's good to have the opportunity to have this kind of long-term commitment.

I mean, we could also at any point just walk out of here. If we get totally tired, we could just walk out. It wouldn't be a big problem. Then we'll have to find the transition. But I'm sure people would be happy to take it over. This is not a burden. It's a responsibility and we really take it, but it's not like a burden.

Do you think you are running this place because you feel responsible for the society, somehow? Or it's mostly for yourself that you want to do it?

I think this is why we do work in the public space. This is why we are interested in creating interaction between the local community and artists. Because I think we feel it's good to take some responsibility for society, not just for yourself. I mean, it's quite boring just to take responsibility for yourself. And this is also question of age. I fully understand that the longer you live in a society, and maybe you start to appreciate certain aspects of your society that you live in, the more you want to take responsibility.

You think like, hey, I'm still here. Nothing really bad has happened to me, wow. And this is due to the fact that people took responsibility, you know. You start to understand your life is what it is because other people took responsibility and developed a place you liked and you went to, and so on. So you feel like, ok, is it a good feeling to also give something back? To take responsibility, it's a good feeling.

What about the residencies here in Berlin? I know there are a lot of residencies here. Can you give me an overview of the landscape, and what kind of differences there are between these residencies?

Basically, the residencies in Berlin… there is one residency which is funded by the federal government. It's called Bethanien. That's the only one that's federally funded. All the other ones are running on basically renting the space out to artists. Of course there is like *DAAD*, you know, stuff like that, but it's not a residency in that sense.

And maybe some art schools they also have studios. And also, other countries rent studios. Like, Switzerland has a lot of studios spread out all over Berlin, and they send Swiss artist to their studios. But it's not a residency in that sense. It's more like a scholarship, but it's a residency in the sense that you live and work somewhere. *DAAD* is funded by the federal government of Deutschland, and they have a different model. Artists from all over the world can come here and get funded by this scholarship, and they get a studio.

Then other spaces, there are many smaller

spaces, they rent their space out to institutions and to artists directly.

Speaking of the funding system for the residencies, how much funding support is out there for artists here? What are the chances that artists can actually get some funding?

From their local governments. You know, it really depends on where you come from. So if you come from Canada there is a good chance, if you come from Australia there is a good chance, because they have a lot of cultural and travel funding. There are other countries where it's much more difficult. We have an artist here right now from Nigeria, and the Goethe-Institute is funding him to come here. So it totally depends, there is no general answer to this.

How good is the chance? It really depends on where you stand as an artist in your career and how solid your work is. It depends on your local funding structures. And also… I mean it's kind of difficult for younger artists, because they don't have this kind of solid work. This is always the problem for younger artists. So we've also won funds that allow us to give somebody a green card, say you can come and we pay for it. There's one residency that we do this with.

So you were saying for younger artists it's more difficult, but also doing residencies is kind of necessary for artists now to take off in their career.

It's part of your career, part of your CV, and if it's not in your CV, then it will be a bit difficult for you. Yeah, yeah, it's tricky. You have to get into this system. You know, this kind of first step into the system where you go on one, or maybe two residencies, then from there your network develops, your CV grows, you develop your work, it's paid. If you get into this thing, then it gets easier and easier. Until you are 40, and nobody will take you anymore. (Laugh)

I heard that for a lot of them, the cap is 35.

Yeah yeah, it's true. Definitely, we are still travelling a lot not because we go on residencies, but because we get invited a lot. I mean, we haven't applied for any travel stuff for 10 years now. Yeah, because we couldn't, 35. (laugh)

For your artist collective part, do you also have to promote it somehow, or let other people know what you are doing?

Sure. In the year 2015, you have to communicate, day and night. Yeah sure, we do communicate what we do, because our work also relies a lot on communication. Yeah, we have Twitter. *ZK/U* has Twitter. Of course we communicate in all these different channels what we do.

And people just see that, and they want to invite you?

Yeah, and mostly people invite us because they know us from personal connections. And this is also kind of a tricky part for youngsters to get into this market. Somebody seeing your work is not enough. It happens also, but not very often.

Usually what happens is like, one of us goes to panel talks, and presents a work, and then somebody says 'wow'. The work starts talking to you, and then this is the first meeting. And you have some second meeting in a different place, or they happen to be in Berlin, and then things develop.

Of course, over time, your address book gets bigger. You know more people. It's how it is. So, in the beginning, it's really difficult. And this is also why, and I think this is really right, these kind of travel grants are limited to a certain age. Of course not all travel grants are like this. There are travel grants in the world where they take 60-year-old artists, because of the diversity. And we also realize this, having a diverse mix of artists in the residencies is super, it's the best. You have to have some older, you have to have some younger artists. And then it gets really good. If the age group is too homogeneous, it's not good. It's really like, the dynamic gets really negative. You start having fights. Yeah, it's really interesting. This is a social experiment.

So throughout your artistic career, what kind of jobs have you done along the way to make money?

Starting with doing regular jobs in bars, of course. And working for radio stations, TV stations, odd jobs, that was while I was studying, and through the transition phase, from finishing my study to working independently, I was in a very lucky position.

While I was studying, I was playing music and composing. I started doing this when I was 16. And then, I was able to actually really make some money with this. I got royalties from compositions that I made. So this helped me for like 3 years to get through this phrase, where I didn't really have to work, where I could do my artistic work. Lucky. I was still doing music videos. This was sort of after I came out of art school. So I made some money there. And media animation jobs 'cause I studied experimental film, so I was an After Effects operator. Editor, editor for films. Directing for music videos. So this was like maybe 5 years from when I was 29 until I was 34.

And since then, I've never done any jobs except for teaching… and I'm still doing this today. Teaching in the art context. Teaching at art schools. I was teaching at *UDK, University of Art in Berlin*. And 2 years ago I had a professorship for 1 year as a guest professor at *Kassel University,* where the *Documenta* is.

You were a musician before?

Yeah, yeah, I was. It was part time, part time artistic activity.

How old were you then?

I started being a musician when I was 16, and I had my first record contract when I was 19. And I played music on a semi-professional level while I was in art school. During my art school time I was also playing in different bands, composing music for other people. So, it was half of my time with this, and half of my time with art studies.

And after I graduated I still continued doing some of that, and actually some money came in. Then I came to the point where I had to decide where I put my time. Do I put my time into music, or art?

And my girlfriend got pregnant. I had to make life decisions. I really said, stop that music thing. It's youth culture, it's gonna be sad when you are 40, and you didn't really fully succeed. And in the art world, you can grow old in decency. It was really like a decision time. I started to do art. I'm happy with this decision.

And now you get a salary here to pay yourself?

Yeah, we get some kind of basic salary. And the rest of the money comes from doing art projects from the outside, and comes from doing workshops also.

Your life is well lived!

Yeah, it never got boring, this much I can say. But it was also very intense. And it's going to continue like this. I'm not tired. Yeah, I feel up for it.

www.zku-berlin.org
www.kunstrepublik.de

Matthias，43岁，柏林

2015年8月27日
采访于柏林Moabit区

我从你们网站上了解了这个地方的一些信息，但是我想听一听更个人化角度的故事，你是怎么开始做这些的？这个地方是怎么运作的？首先请自我介绍一下吧。

我叫做Matthias。我是ZK/U（柏林艺术与城市化中心）的三个负责人之一，也是艺术家组合KUNSTrePUBLIK的四位成员之一。这两个身份是有交叉的。KUNSTrePUBLIK（艺术共和小组）的成员和ZK/U的负责人是同一群人，除了一位住在汉堡的KUNSTrePUBLIK成员没有参与ZK/U的项目外。我们运营ZK/U已经有三年时间了。ZK/U是2012年8月开始的。在那之前，我们几个人已经在一起工作了8年。所以我们其实已经在一起工作很长时间了。

我们开始时以艺术家小组的方式一起在公共空间做项目，在世界各地做项目。当然最主要还是在柏林。我们逐渐意识到我们需要有一个稳定的基地。不仅是在柏林，我猜所有的大城市都一样，存在着市区以内房租不断上涨的问题。作为艺术家，我们没有非常高昂的收入，所以我们需要找到可以继续留在这个城市里的办法。于是，我们开始寻找一个能让我们可持续地工作和生活的地方。这是大概6年前的事了。然后，有一天我们经过了这幢建筑，我们意识到它太大了，不可能只是给我们自己用，我们需要为其他人也创造些什么。再加上其他种种原因，我们就开始了运营这个驻留项目的计划。

ZK/U基本上分为两个部分。一个是公共的部分，另一个是私人的部分。私人部分意味着我们有14个驻留空间，来自全世界的艺术家在这里工作和生活。驻留时间从2个月到8个月不等。我们关注围绕城市环境主题进行创作的艺术家，思考并提问“城市可以是什么样的”，“城市如何被它过去的历史所影响”，“来自世界各地的影响如何改变一个城市”。所以我们试图把在这一领域工作的艺术家们聚集到一起。不光是艺术家，还有以科学研究方式工作的人，比如社会学家，建筑师，设计师等，以及那些和社会参与有关的人。我们的想法和关注重点就是——“城市话语”。

另外，我们也尝试在当地的社群活动和来自世界各地的艺术家的活动中间找到平衡和联接。这通常是挺困难的。通常你会看到艺术家在驻留空间做他们自己的事，然后他们在画廊有一个开放日展览什么的。但是驻留艺术家和他实际所在的周围驻留环境并没有互动。所以这是我们想要关注的地方。因此，我们这幢楼的第二个部分，也就是我们现在所在的公共空间，另外还有大堂即展览大厅，和楼下的地窖，这些公共空间都是用来做各种活动的。

我们有开放日，每两周举行一次实验跳蚤市集，每周五有实验电影放映，放映精心挑选的影片和美食，美食都是和那天放映的电影相关的。另外我们还举行各种各样的工作坊，研讨会和展览。各种不光对艺术圈和城市科学研究方面的人有吸引力，而且本地的普通观众也可能会有兴趣的活动。因为这样能在公众和艺术家们的兴趣中间创造张力。艺术家有时候宁愿只是在画廊里做他们的展览，或是只想呆在艺术的小圈子里。而普通的大众有时候又只想要非常简单而不用太实验的形式。所以我们试图在这两者之间找到平衡。这样人们就可以真的参与进来而不用觉得他们完全来错了地方。要调和得好并不容易，但是我们觉得这样的桥梁是值得去搭建的。

你是怎么开始想要做这件事的？这个机构空间和你之前做艺术家小组的经验有什么关系吗？

没错。作为艺术家小组，我们一直都很有兴趣发展那些社会互动性的作品。我们主要在公共空间里创作。我们从来也没真的在画廊或美术馆那样的空间做过展览。我们的作品都是非常场地特定的，并且和当地的社群发生互动。

作品的成形都有一个过程。我们从来不会突然冒出来一个想法，接着开始执行这个想法，然后就结束了。我们的过程总是：先一起去一个地方，做一些研究调查，先了解一下这里到底是什么情况，再开始从中发展作品。然后两个月以后我们发展出让社群中每个人都可以参与进来的项目。这就是我们如何创作的过程。因为我们认为，艺术不仅仅是形式和信息，还可以是过程和社会性的互动。

听上去你们的作品好像和大地艺术或公共艺术相关。但是当你说你们不在画廊展出的时候，是因为你们的作品不是画廊会卖的类型，所以他们不愿意展你呢？还是说你们故意做这些不能在画廊展出的作品来作为一种艺术态度？

两个都是。真的。一方面，我们不做易于售卖的作品。我是说，我们也做录像和摄影。但是那些对于艺术市场来说并没有什么吸引力。我们并不是说："不，我们绝不卖任何东西给任何人。"这不是说我因为很在乎艺术市场，所以我对它有很强的喜恶。只是刚好我们互相都觉得彼此没有什么吸引力，真的是这样。

对我来说这非常有意思，因为通常艺术家如果想要拥有一个职业生涯，他们会需要把自己委身于这个艺术系统来被认证，被认可。

对，那挺不容易的。

但是听上去你现在在这里所做的事，你创建了自己的系统，这有点像是一个机构，但又不是一个真正的机构。

是的，没错。我们从来也没试图要成为一个传统意义上的机构。我们做很多事，而且它也变得越来越像一个机构了，不管我们是不是喜欢这样。我们现在有一个10个人的团队。哦，不止，有14个人。加上驻留的艺术家就差不多有20人。所以基本上总是至少有14个人在这里。你可以在一定程度上有机地管理它，但是你也需要开始思考组织架构。否则，你知道，很多事情总是在重复发生。

艺术家来到这里以后，他们想要知道这里的基本结构是怎么样的，我们能为他们做些什么。当他们需要这些东西的时候要上哪儿才能找到。你知道，一开始的时候跟他们解释和介绍这些还挺新鲜的，但是过了一阵之后，就会有很多重复性的事，然后我们也希望能更多地把重心放到内容上。我们会想要更多关注策展，和艺术家们一起发展想法。所以这些结构性的事你就会想要把它机构化。这是很自然的发展过程。

不过话说回来，我们的整个结构，我们有三个主理人，这其实是个笑话。我们三个人一起建立了这个地方，我们试图把团队内部的结构保持扁平化，没有人想要当财务傻逼，每个人都想要只负责艺术性方面的工作。但是我们必须共同分担这些工作。

在三年时间里，你们从创始的 3 个人成长到现在有10个人以上的团队，外加艺术家。这一切是怎么发生的？尤其是财务方面，你们是怎么做到的？收入从哪里来呢？

没问题，我可以解释一下。基本上，我们建造这个地方没需要花一分钱。因为这部分的开销是有赞助的。这幢楼的内部基本上是全新的。而装修的钱是由不同的基金支持的。我们当时需要160万欧元来重新装修整幢楼。我们拿到了钱。所以我们没有银行贷款需要偿还，这让我们有一个比较好的处境。

然后，基本上我们的驻留项目以两种不同的方式来运作。驻留项目为我们带来收入。一方面，我们和租用我们空间的机构签订合同，然后他们再把空间提供给艺术家使用。比如，我们有一个韩国的机构合作夥伴，他们租用了一个空间，他们会给我们提供他们觉得适合ZK/U项目的艺术家名单，然后我们再从中选择最终会过来驻留的艺术家。

这是一部分，另外一部分是我们的开放式邀请。任何人都可以申请，如果我们喜欢你的作品，我们会给你发送你所需要的所有文件来帮助你申请能够支持你驻留的国家性或地方性基金。比如一位加拿大艺术家会拿到一份邀请说，“我们邀请你……”然后他们会告诉我们，“啊，写研究和展览。”所以我们就按照艺术家的要求来写，然后他再把邀请递交给当地的基金申请渠道。在收到我们的邀请之后，艺术家有三年的时间去寻找基金支持。这样他们的驻留费用就由当地的艺术支持结构承担了。所以这是两个最主要的驻留方式。

另外我们也有一些过来参加驻留的学者，他们有一学期的休假。而且他们也有充足的收入。所以他们就自己付租金。这些收入基本上就帮助我们维持这幢建筑的运营和我们在这里做的各种活动，差不多是这样。但这些钱并不够，因为这幢楼的维护开销还挺大的。所以我们也需要通过出租场地给其他想要在这做展览的机构来盈收。不过这其实挺难平衡的，因为我们真的需要看一下这些活动符不符合我们的项目安排理念，会不会差太多。所以我们总是需要非常小心地来做决定。这是一个策展的问题。

但是目前为止这些活动都还平衡地不错？

是的，差不多吧。总也会有高低起伏。但是我对目前我们的项目发展都还挺满意的。驻留项目的部分，有时候会有些小困难。我们在驻留项目上花了很多心血，比如我们每周都有晚餐聚会和作品展示，我们会有策展人过来拜访，还为艺术家提供每个月做一次展览的机会和开放日活动。所以艺术家们可以决定他们是只想在工作室里工作，还是想要拿出来展览。

但是我们所提供的越多，艺术家们就越需要我们的个人化注意力。这当然很正常。因为他们不了解这里的结构等等。但是这些其实都需要花钱，因为我们得付钱请人来做这些事。所以你付出越多，越想做好，就会越花钱。当然，你也会碰到越多问题和误解等等。所以这就变得越来越复杂。不过这也是事情开始变得有趣的时候。

作为这个空间的负责人，你的一天或一周是怎么分配的？

这也是有点难的部分。因为我们其实同时也还在做很多艺术方面的创作，我们也还经常旅行。比如我们最近在俄罗斯做一个项目，所以需要离开4周。这种情况就挺困难了。如果我们不在这，很多事情就真的很难管理。所以我们需要把这些都安排地非常好。以一周的节奏来说，我会有四天时间在这里工作。然后我会花一天加上周末的时间来做些我自己的事，像是艺术性的项目，或是仅仅用来安排我的生活。如果你是独立地工作而不是给别人打工的话，你会需要花很多时间来安排自己的生活。所以这可能就得花上一周里的两天时间。剩下还有一天我可能什么都不做就在湖边呆着放松一下。

但是你还有7个人以上的员工，你需要管理他们吗？需要告诉他们做什么吗？比如项目的运营，或是安排如何运转这个地方的其他具体工作？

是的。我们会有一些重复出现的工作，会有一些日常工作。所以这些部分就不需要再跟他们说了，他们自己会处理。比如我们的活动联络人，我们的驻留联络人，他们知道怎样制定合同，如何和大众沟通等等。但是除此以外的其他事也挺多的，我们总会需要大家一起坐下来讨论。

我们每周一都会有一个团队例会，每次2–4个小时，还挺长时间的。但是这是非常重要的让团队里的每个人都知道现在空间里在发生什么的机会。当然，在某种程度上，我们的确需要“指导”，但仅仅是在一定程度上。我们的雇员在工作中有很多自由做决定的机会。财务方面，我们还是需要掌握大局。但是收入方面基本上也还相对稳定，需要支付的工资和其他基本开销也是基本固定的。

通常对于艺术家来说，他们都只要管好自己一个人就行了。但是你们可能已经习惯了以小组团队的方式合作工作。而这个地方又挺大的，很多事情在这里发生，也需要很大的责任。再加上这又是一个非常长期的承诺，决定把精力放到这件事上，让它发生和实现。

对，是这样。我们现在也不完全确定现在这样是不是真的是我们想要的。你知道，我们在这做了很多有意思的事。我们也有很多自由，可以做决定。这都很棒。但是行政性的部分又确实占很大比重。所以我有时候真的怀疑，我们真的还有足够的时间来做艺术项目吗？这当然是个问题。目前为止，我们都还挺幸运的。每年我们都有机会做项目，好几个项目。但是长期来说，这确实挺有压力的。我们非常非常努力地工作来维持这里艺术性和行政性工作的基本需求。我也不会说我们会永远这样继续下去。

我不介意也许几年以后，当这个地方的运转变得足够稳定，那时候我们就可以慢慢地平稳退出。也许我可以作为顾问董事，每个月就过来一次。但是现在还不是时候，我们还有很多基础性的工作要做。我觉得可能会需要再过5-10年这里的运转才会变得真正稳定。

关于你的第一个问题。是的，我们非常习惯一起工作。我现在也还在和另外两个艺术小组一起做项目。我也做个人项目，但是我更喜欢以艺术小组的方式合作，那样更有趣。我喜欢这样的社会性互动。这些都挺好的，我很喜欢。而且这对我很有帮助。一个人不会总有很棒的想法。总也有些时候你会没什么灵感。然后你就卡壳了。但如果是在艺术小组里，其他成员就能启发你。所以这非常有帮助。你就不会陷入这种艺术家的创作危机。

作为一个个体，你会陷入非常深的危机。我以前独自作为艺术家工作的时候曾有过那样的阶段，我会觉得，我到底在做什么呀？太糟糕了，我的作品不够好。但是在一个艺术组合里，你可以依赖彼此，那样更有意思。而且我觉得开始考虑我们作为一个艺术组合，如何慢慢地淡出这个机构并让年轻的一代来继续发展它，那其实是更健康的思考方式。因为作为组合，我们也需要改变。而新的挑战是非常重要的。我觉得这也是把我们继续联接在一起的原因。你会碰到全新的挑战，并迎接挑战。这是加强我们关系的纽带。

建立并运营这个空间也是你们艺术小组的艺术申明吗？

是的。我们把它当作我们的艺术项目的一部分。你知道，像这样的项目，以及我们是如何发展它的，这其中的故事非常曲折。我不觉得任何正常人会想要经历这样的过程来创建这个地方。没有人，没有一个投资人会做这样的事。一个建筑师不会做这件事，任何生意人都不会想做这件事。我觉得正因为它是一件这么不合常理的事，而且是非常难做的事。所以我们真的冒着很大的风险开始来做这件事。

这个地方以前是个火车站吗？

是的。

它属于政府吗？

以前是，但是现在它是属于我们的了。我们作为机构KUNSTrePUBLIK拥有这个地方。这是为什么它这么复杂的原因。也是为什么我们花这么多精力在这幢建筑上。这是一个非常有意思的结构。这幢楼所在的土地属于柏林市政府。

所以市政府拥有土地，但我们拥有房屋。而这又是公共公园的一部分，任何人都可以进来。我们有这幢楼所在土地的租约。租约的年限是37年，一旦合同到期，柏林市政府可以说，“我们要收回这块土地。”这在37年后是可能发生的。如果那时他们想要我们搬到别的地方，那他们就会需要付给KUNSTrePUBLIK一笔钱来偿付这幢楼到时所值的价钱。所以这样的情况对我们来说是非常幸运的。

但是另一方面，我觉得这也很有意思，因为当地政府确实可以施加影响。37年后，他们可以说，这个地方已经不再相关了。我觉得这其实对我们来说是一个很好的角度。因为37年后，我们双方都可以再次做一个决定。我觉得这是好事。通常，土地一旦卖给私有公司或者私人拥有者之后，城市就再也不能对这块土地的规划施加任何影响。一旦它卖出就永远收不回来了。但是以我们的例子来说，我们双方都可以再做一次决定。

这样的合同是非常复杂的。要起草这样的合同，并且从法律的角度找到一个成立的基础是非常复杂的。

但是37年是挺长的一段时间，是什么让你决定要投身于此呢？

你知道，我们一直都在做一些我们也不知道一年或两年之后会发展成什么样的项目。但是柏林的现实情况是，如果你找不到稳定的场地，那么早晚你会因为房租上涨而被赶出去。作为一名艺术家，你能变成非常有名的画廊艺术家的概率是非常非常小的。这是很多学艺术的学生都没有看到的现实。在德国，能成为艺术家，把艺术当作你的工作的可能性是2%。所以当你去上艺术院校的时候，只有2%的学生以后会能在艺术领域工作。通过售卖作品或成为策展人来谋生的概率只有2%。剩下的98%会去从事完全不同的行业。

或是在一段时间内，他们能获得一些艺术基金资助，但是同时也还需要另一份工作。

没错，直到那另一份工作变成了主业。（笑）事情就是这样。有数据统计调查了艺术学生毕业十年以后的就业情况。所以这就是现实，痛苦的现实。

所以我们也意识到，我们必须要找到一个更持久的模式。一会儿在这里做个项目，一会儿在那里做个项目，很快我们就不得不中止艺术项目而去做些奇怪的工作来谋生了，要不就是变成老师。

你可能还会用得上一些你所学过的知识。但是你会不得不做一份艺术以外的工作。我们意识到柏林特殊的情形非常复杂，而且正在变得越来越艰难。所以我们逼着自己找一个相对长期的地方。而且有机会做这样一个长期的承诺对我们来说也是一个很好的机会。

我是说，任何时候我们其实都可以走开不干了。如果我们完全累垮了，我们可以大不了就不干了。那不会是个很大的问题。那时候我们就需要找到过渡。不过我很确定会有人很愿意接手。这不是一个累赘，而是一份责任。而我们是真的把这份责任承担下来了。

你在运营这个空间是因为某种程度上你觉得对社会应该负有责任吗？还是主要因为你自己想要做这件事？

我觉得这正是我们为什么在公共空间创作的原

因。这也正是为什么我们有兴趣在当地社群和艺术家之间建立互动关系的原因。因为我们觉得为社会，而不仅仅是为自己去承担一些责任是特别好的事。这和年纪也有关系。我完全理解当你在这个社会上活的越久，也许你就会开始感激你所在社会的某些方面，你也就越想要承担责任。

你会觉得，“嘿，我还在这呢。没有什么特别糟糕的事在我身上发生。而这是因为有人承担了责任。”你开始理解你的生活之所以能像现在这样，是因为其他人承担了责任并建立了一个你喜欢的地方。所以你会开始觉得，如果我也能回馈些什么会不会是很好的感觉？承担责任，是一种非常好的感觉。

我知道柏林有很多驻留空间。你可以给我大概介绍一下这些空间的情况吗？这些驻留项目之间有什么区别吗？

基本上，柏林的驻留项目。只有一个是完全由联邦政府出资支持的。叫做Bethanien。那是唯一仅有的一个。所有其他的驻留基本上都是靠出租空间给艺术家的模式来运营。当然还有DAAD一类的政府基金（德意志学术交流中心），但它并不是单纯的驻留项目。

可能有些艺术院校也有工作室。另外有些国家也在柏林租用工作室提供给来自他们国家的艺术家。比如瑞士就在柏林有很多工作室，他们把瑞士艺术家送来这里。但那也并不是真正意义上的驻留，更像是一个奖学金。不过，也可以说它是驻留，因为你还是在另一个地方工作和生活了。DAAD是由德意志联邦政府资助的，他们有另一种运营模式。来自全世界各地的艺术家都可以申请该奖学金来柏林，并获得一个工作室。

除此以外其他的一些空间都相对较小，他们直接向机构或艺术家出租空间。

说到驻留项目的基金赞助系统，你知道有多少基金可以申请吗？艺术家能真的拿到奖助的机会又有多少？

大多数艺术基金是通过艺术家当地的政府获得的。你知道，这真得得取决于你所来自的国家。如果你来自加拿大和澳大利亚，那你就会有很多机会。因为他们有很多文化和旅行的艺术基金。而其他的国家就可能会困难地多。我们现在这里有一个驻留艺术家来自尼日利亚，歌德学院就赞助了他来这里的驻留。所以这完全得看情况而定，并没有一个一概而论的答案。

有多大的机率可以拿到奖助？这得看你作为一名艺术家的职业发展到了什么程度，以及你的作品有多扎实。这也取决于你所在地区的基金支持系统。另外，对于年轻艺术家来说，申请总是不那么容易的。因为他们的作品发展地还不够成熟。这对于年轻艺术家来说总是个问题。所以我们也申请到了一个基金可以让我们能够给特别优秀的艺术家发一张通关卡，说，“你可以过来，我们会为你支付费用。”我们有一个驻留的名额是这样的。

你是说驻留项目对年轻艺术家来说是比较难申请的，但却又是艺术家职业发展必经的一个步骤？

驻留是你职业发展的一部分，也是你简历的一部分。如果你简历上没有这些经历，那你的艺术生涯就会更艰难一些，所以这是很矛盾的。你需要进入这个系统。像这样的驻留是帮你进入艺术系统的第一步，你先开始一两个驻留，然后从那开始慢慢发展你的社交网络，你的简历也会随之丰富，你发展自己的作品，开始有人付钱买你的作

品。一旦你进入了系统，就会变得越来越容易。一直到你40岁，那时就再也没人会接受你的驻留了。（笑）

我听说很多项目的申请年龄上限是35岁？

是的是的。没错。我们现在之所以还能经常旅行，不是因为我们去参加驻留，而是因为我们被邀请参加展览和活动。我们已经有10年没申请过旅行基金了。是的，因为我们申请不了了。已经过了35岁。（笑）

关于你们的艺术家小组，你们需要自己去推广它吗？让其他人知道你们在做什么？

当然了。在2015年，你不得不昼夜不分地去交流和沟通。我们当然需要让人知道我们在做什么，因为我们的作品本来就很大程度上需要依赖于沟通。我们有twitter。ZK/U也有twitter。我们会通过所有这些不同的渠道去让人知道我们在做什么。

人们看到你们的宣传，然后就想要邀请你们吗？

是的。不过大多数时候人们邀请我们是因为他们已经通过私交关系先认识了我们。而这也是年轻人要进入这一市场所要面对的困难之一。仅仅有人看到你的作品还不够。当然那样的情况也发生过，不过并不常见。

通常是，我们几个人中的某个人去参加一场研讨会讲演，介绍了我们的作品，然后有人会觉得很不错。我们的作品开始和人们产生沟通。这一般是初次会面。然后你们又会在另外一个什么地方碰到，或者他们刚好在柏林。然后慢慢地很多事情就会有所进展。

当然，时间久了，你的通讯录也会变厚。你也认识了更多的人。事情就是这样的。但是，一开始的时候会非常困难。而这也是为什么这些旅行基金会有年龄限制，我觉得其实是对的。当然不是所有的旅行基金都是这样。有些基金出于多元化的需要也会接受60岁艺术家的申请。而我们也意识到，有多元化，不同背景的艺术家来参加驻留项目是非常棒的，这是最好的情况。有年长的艺术家，有年轻的艺术家，这样就会非常好。如果艺术家的年龄太接近了并不是好事，气氛会变得挺糟糕，会开始有人打架。所以这挺有趣的，就像一个社会实验一样。

在你的艺术生涯中，你还做过些什么别的工作来挣钱吗？

当然一开始的时候就是在酒吧做一些常见的工作。后来我在电台和电视台也都干过，还做过一些其他乱七八糟的工作。那都是在我还在上学的时候。

当我还在学校的时候，我就做音乐并作曲。我16岁的时候就开始做这些。后来，我居然真的靠音乐挣了些钱。我可以拿我音乐作曲的版权费。那笔钱帮助我渡过了三年的过渡时期，让我可以在那段时间不用工作，而只是专注在我的艺术创作上。真的很幸运。另外我也还做过媒体动画的工作。因为我学过实验电影，所以我也做过影视特效师，电影剪辑师，也导演过MV。这是从我29岁到34岁中间的差不多五年时间。

34岁之后，我就除了教书以外再也没有做过任何其他工作。现在我也还在艺术院校教书。我在柏林艺术大学教过。两年前，我还在卡塞尔大学当过一年的客座教授。

你以前还是音乐人？

是的。我曾经是。那只是我业余时间做的。

你那时候多大？

我是16岁的时候开始做音乐的。19岁的时候我就拿到了第一张唱片的合同。我在美院的时候也一直以半专业的水准在做音乐。那时候我同时在几个不同的乐队演出，也给其他人作曲。所以，我有一半的时间都在做音乐，另一半时间在学习艺术。

毕业以后，我也还接着做一些音乐。居然还挣到了些钱。再后来，到了一个阶段，我不得不在如何分配自己的时间上做个决定。我是把时间放在音乐上还是艺术上呢？然后那时候我女朋友又怀孕了。我真的对自己说，“放下那些音乐的事吧。那只是年轻人的文化。等你到了40岁，那时如果你也没有获得真正的成功会很惨的。而在艺术的世界，你可以优雅地变老。”那时真的是必须作出决定的时候。最终，我选择了艺术。我很开心我做了这个决定。

现在在这里你给自己发工资吗？

是的，我们有一份基本工资。其他的收入就通过我们在外面做艺术项目和工作坊。

你的生命过得太充实了！

是的，我从来没觉得无聊过。这是我可以说的。但是也一直都非常紧张激烈。未来也会继续如此。我不觉得累。没错，我很乐意迎接挑战。

www.zku-berlin.org
www.kunstrepublik.de

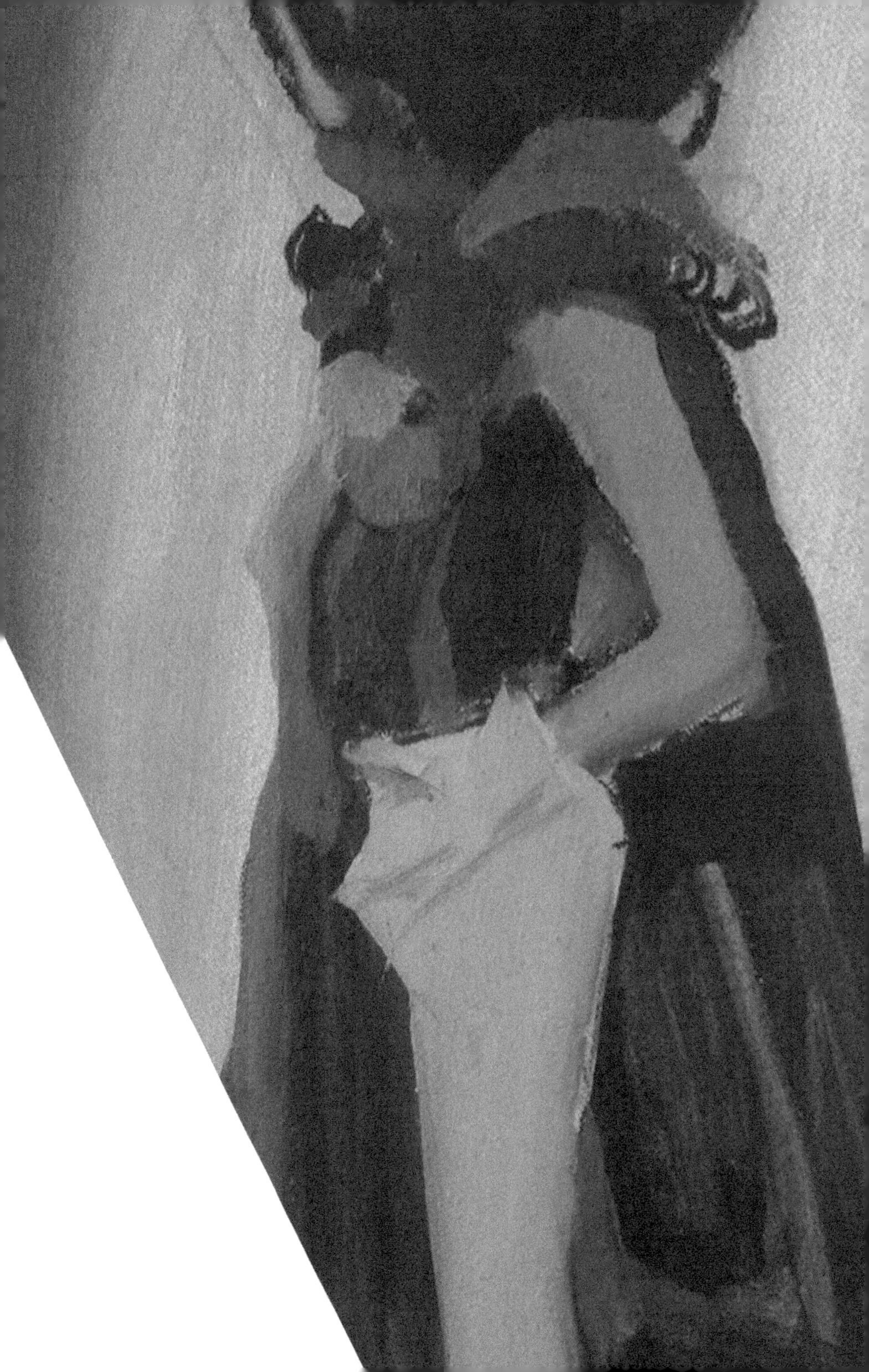

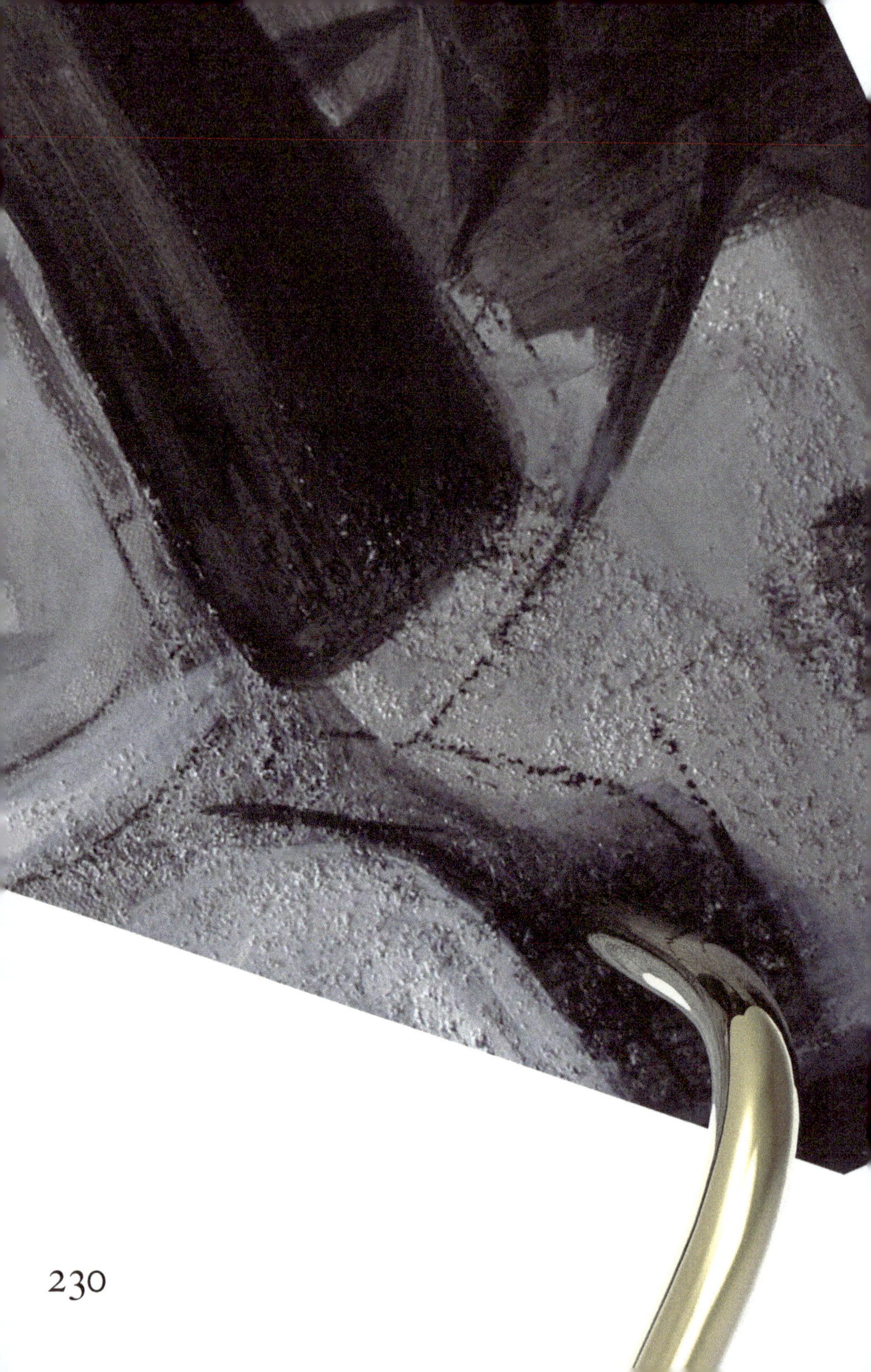

Zoë, Berlin

Interviewed in Kreuzberg, Berlin
August 25th, 2015

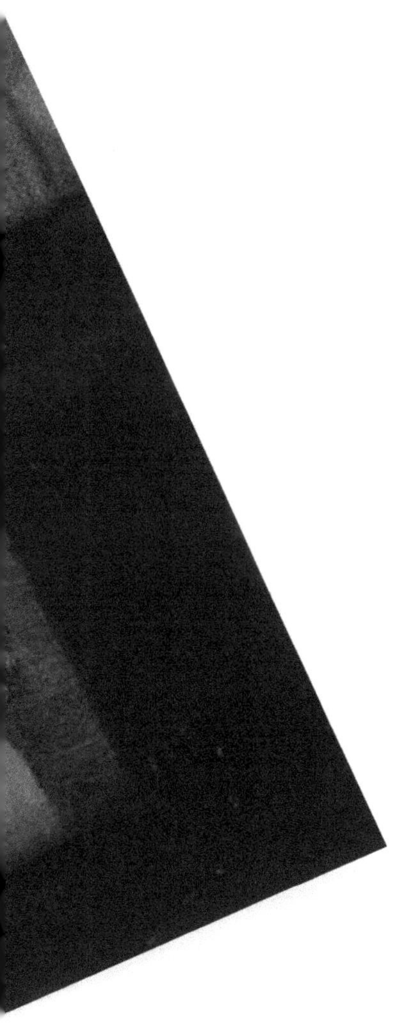

Please introduce yourself.

My name is *Zoë Claire Miller*. I have been living in Berlin for 7 years and I'm an artist/organizer. Some of my largest recent projects have been *the Berlin Art Prize*, which is an artist-funded and artist-run independent art prize, and *the Time Grants Campaign*, which is a campaign to enact more public funding for the arts in Berlin.

Can you talk a little bit more about *the Berlin Art Prize*?

The Berlin Art Prize was founded in 2013 by *Alicia Reuter* and *Sophie Jung*, who are both writers/art historians, and *Ulrich Wulff* and I – we are both artists. And the idea came about because we felt like it was kind of a sad state in Berlin that there are so many artists, I mean, a really huge population of artists, over 10,000, and so few art prizes that seem to be doing something interesting, or that show the viewer something exciting.

It seemed like everything was either institutional invite-only elitism or pure corporate vaunt. Like *Vattenfall*, who has a monopoly on energy and provides electricity in Berlin. They had their prize, and it was completely about their prestige, and not about supporting the arts. And all the institutional and city prizes seem to always go to very very predictable candidates. They were all the kind of awards that you got if you were already really successful in the art market.

There are publicly funded art grants rather than prizes but there are so few of them, and they really weren't accompanied by good presswork or by visibility. So it's kind of like, oh you can look up, if you spend half an hour on the city administration's non-user-friendly website, you might be able to find the 15 people who got this award from the Berlin Senate in a given year.

We were really interested in the whole

construct of how quality is declared, how reputation is built up. It always seems like it's a very hierarchical top-to-bottom kind of system where those who have a lot of prestige and money are ready to declare, 'Ok, I shared some of my power and prestige on you and by that I raise you up.' 'Cause that's usually the way it goes.

You know, if you are young and you want to make it as an artist, you have to find people in positions of power who are willing to support your work. If your personality is unsuited to Darwinian competition and self-promotion, then good luck with that.

And we kind of wanted to turn that around, to make it like a very accurate cover version of an art prize, with all of the classical aspects, but coming from a very different place, and in a kind of subversive spirit.

So it's composed of a group show with around 30 nominees, so people who are nominated are all exhibited. And each year, three artists win. And what they win is prize money, which usually isn't much, because we have no funding. So it's just kind of like what's left over after we've paid off other bills. And most of the money we generate through selling drinks at the big opening party, but also through donations, and we have a lot of amazing local sponsors who give us very good deals, or print things for free, or support us with material.

But yeah, the prize money is mainly thought to cover the cost of the residency, so they are not supposed to pay any money out of their pocket. And they get a residency each year in a different country. The first year was in Italy, last year was in Georgia, and this year, it's in Greece.

So the prize itself doesn't really have money, but basically you have to wait till the opening day to generate money?

Yes, it's not a very ideal situation. It also

leaves us all in the air, and super worried about whether we will make enough money, and if not, what we do. Last year we didn't make enough money, so we did another party later in the year to make the funds that we are missing, but it's really a pity that the city isn't willing to support the prize at all. Because I feel like we've gotten a lot of, and generated a lot of good publicity for Berlin and Berlin's artists.

Oh, but I forgot one important aspect of the Prize also is the trophy. So you get a beautiful trophy and it's made by different artists each year. But it's really important for us to really bring people together, and to try to place everyone on a level without regarding all of these kind of aspects that other prizes and competitions have, where you are forcing everyone to do work on some certain subject, or where you say there is an age cut-off, or you have to have a degree in arts, which is really important for us, it's completely inclusive. If you live and work in Berlin, and you've been here for at least half a year, you can apply, and nothing else matters.

On your website, it says this prize is based only on artistic merit. But, what's the standard for artistic merit? Because when you choose together with certain people, there is always this subjective part of it. So how do you choose?

It's always strongly subjective, and it's something that I feel like we cannot put into words at all what artistic merit is. But it's basically the sum of everyone who's working on the prize, and the jury members' opinion of what artistic merit is.

So, there is a different jury every year. And the jury is invited to go through all the nominees, all the applications, and everyone who's working on the team goes through all the nominees, and then, that's how we decide the nominees, and then, the jury alone decides who gets the prize.

But you really do notice that people have very very strong and different opinions at times. Also at times people have absolutely the same opinions so they must have a very synchronized definition of artistic merit. This year, the jury said, 'Oh, we decided within ten minutes who would win when we saw the works.

How many people apply?

Well, on average over the years, I think it's been usually around a thousand applicants.

How much does organizing this prize occupy within your whole working time?

It's very very hard to say, because so much of it is just embedded in other time spent on admin work, like *Berlin Art Prize* emails along with other emails. But it's definitely

3 months of full time work before the exhibition and during the exhibition.

So how do you pay yourself?

No one gets paid at all.

Three to four months full time working on this and no payment?

Yeah, I don't know how we do it either. It's totally insane. I mean that's really the whole thing with *the Berlin Art Prize*. It's like a completely insane idea that was somehow realized. And there are so many parts of it that just seem inexplicable. Like, how can this possibly work out? But this also feels like something that can't continue this way. Because, for me and other people who are most intensely involved, It's also very very emotionally and physically draining, and we all always have burn-out after *the Berlin Art Prize* exhibition

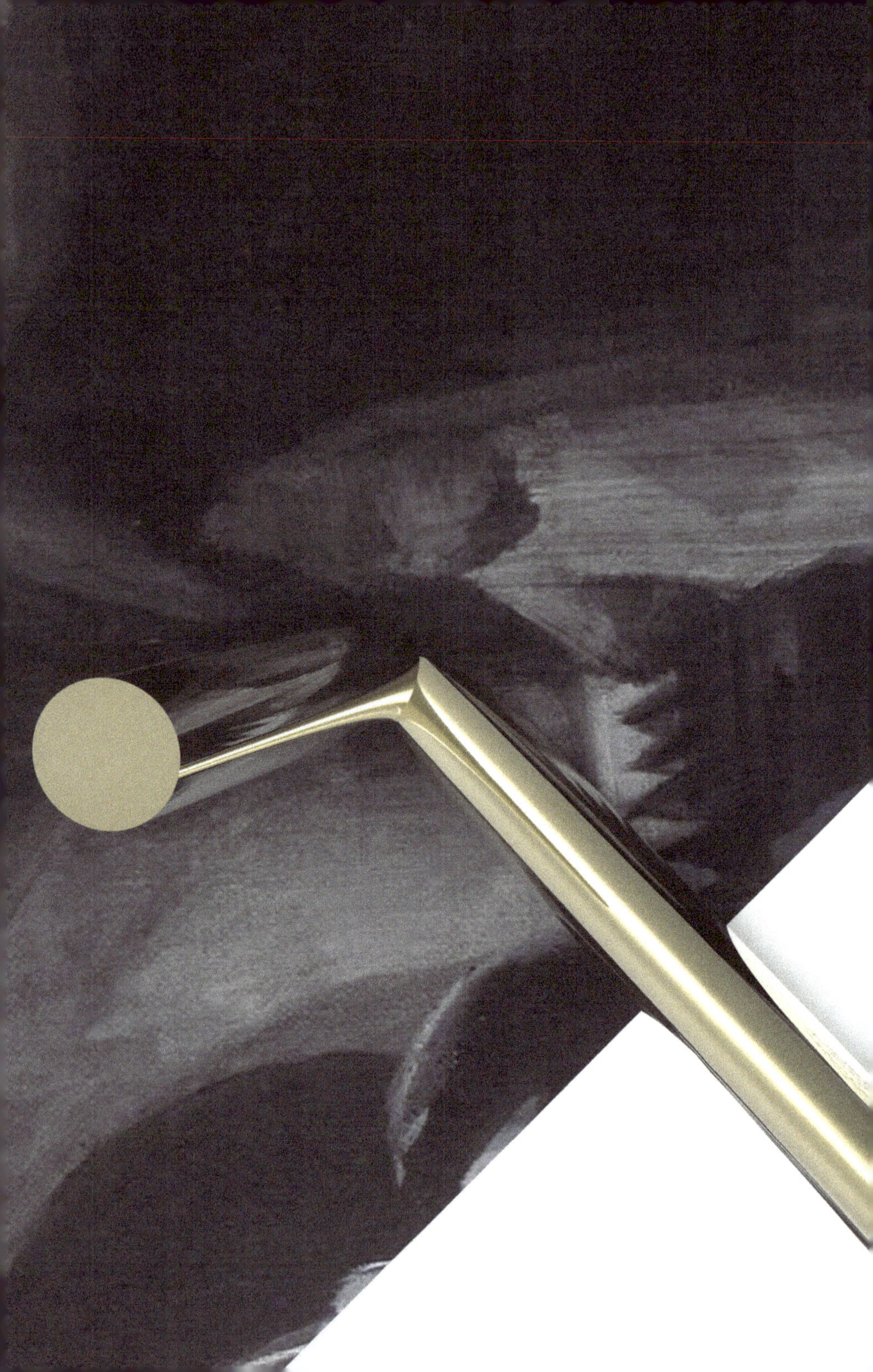

is done. I just feel ruined. And yeah, there has to be a different solution.

So it feels like, you and this group of artists wanted to do something good for the artist community, but without being able to support yourself…

Yeah, I think it really kind of comes down to the whole ridiculous situation of precarity that everyone is in, in some way or another. But I think it's kind of particularly aggravated or extreme in this case. Because the image *the Berlin Art Prize* projects outwards, because we have very good professional graphic design, makes a lot of people who haven't done research think that we have money, that there is magical money coming from somewhere. It's really funny, but it's also tragic.

Are you guys thinking about solutions for the next step?

Yeah, we are. So far we've never gotten any public funding that we've applied for, but I think we can only continue if we get public funding, or we do take on a big main sponsor who really invests in it. Because so far we've always said, 'Oh we don't want to be attached to a big brand name.' But that might be the only way that's possible to continue.

Yeah, that's also tricky. When a brand gives you sponsor money, for one thing, it's like publicity and branding for them. And also, do they really leave you alone to do whatever you want, or do they want to get involved and give you

their opinions?

That's the question. I mean that's why we've always so far wanted to work with a large group of very diverse sponsors and that's always the way that it has been. And they've kind of all had individual desires and needs of what they want to get out of *Berlin Art Prize*, but definitely no one was telling us what to do. It was clear, that was out of the question.

So they just give you some free services?

Yeah.

As you said, one thousand people apply and only three of them get the prize. How do you think those who get turned down should take it?

I think it's more of a comfort that there is so much competition, that then you know… if we had money, if it was possible, every year there are hundreds of people who I think should be nominated. But we have to somehow narrow down to a smaller number. I think it is extremely subjective, and no one should ever be discouraged by rejection, which is obvious so easily said but not done.

At the same time, I do also find it amazing how many artists who do great work are not talented at making portfolios of their work and writing descriptions of their work. And how many artists choose to not write anything about their work. Because we say it's optional, but obviously, certain types of works don't explain themselves very well. And they obviously had a lot of context where it would be very helpful to know.

Every year we also do a class as part of our program with the Art Prize, which is free and open to everyone. We give classes like, 'What's the ideal portfolio?' How can you make things clear to your viewer? And what's the right amount of information, not too much, not too little. Yeah, I feel like also people could ask for help more often. Everyone has friends who are graphic designers, everyone has friends who are art historians who can write text about art. It seems like artists should turn to them more often.

But also of course you always have this really really big divide between the portrayal of the work and then the actual work, which is why it's important for us that the nominated artists turn in their real work, set up their work, and that is shown to the jury before the jury decides who wins. So it's not all only based on a PDF.

Previously, you mentioned that there are ten thousand artists in Berlin. How did you get that number?

In Germany, there is this special kind of retirement/social security that you pay into that is for artists called *KSK*. So they of course know the number of artists. At least they know the number of artists who have been accepted by them. But you have to jump through some hoops. If you are not earning enough money with your art, you can't get into the *KSK*, if you make too much money with other day jobs you can't get in, but if you make it in then the *KSK* basically subsidies the cost of health insurance.

So those ten thousand artists kind of already sell their work somehow?

Yeah, I think often artists who are already successful leave this insurance plan because otherwise they would have to pay high amounts. 'Cause it's based on your income, so if you are earning a lot, you have to pay a lot more. And also, yeah, there are lots and lots of artists who just can't make it in at all, because their works are not commercial enough.

So the actual number might be even bigger?

Oh yeah, for sure. Because also we have to consider everyone who's only here for a while and doesn't really get into this German system, people who have their insurance somewhere else in Europe, or somewhere else in the world, or people who only stay here for a year or two.

What's happening here right now in the Berlin art scene?

I think the most huge recent kind of geographically fixed trend is definitely 'Post-Internet Art', which is now like a démodé term, no one who does 'Post-Internet Art' wants to be called a 'Post-Internet' artist anymore. But a lot of artists who are really working with these themes of technology, branded aesthetics, dystopian, futuristic visions, post-humanism, links to the trendiest theoretical ideas like Accelerationism.

And otherwise, I think there are always very strong kinds of regional styles that you only recognize when you go somewhere else, then you see how different that is from what's going on in the place that you usually are.

For example what would that be?

Well, when you look at things that are going on in the States, or basically New York, that's the most important part for art in the States. You see things that have so many pop-art references that just would not be ok here. People would think that's too pop, too superficial, and that's just like the strongest thing in art history that people refer back to in America, it seems. Whereas here I guess it would be more about other parts of modernism. Something that seemed quintessentially Berlin for a while was a kind of macho, rock'n'roll, bad boy darkness. See the *Guido Baudach gallery*. I would blame this on the weather.

I have the impression that Berlin seems so perfect for art and artists. Is this true? Do you see any problems here?

Oh, there are lots of problems, I mean there are problems everywhere, but some problems that we are definitely facing here is that the cost of living is rising. It's increasingly hard to find affordable workspace. The situation is getting worse and worse for artists living here. I would definitely not recommend to anyone who doesn't have money to move here, it's impossible to find an affordable apartment. And of course, this is the thing everywhere. It's just capitalism combined with irresponsible governance that notices critical issues too late, or just doesn't care.

But for a long time, Berlin held a very

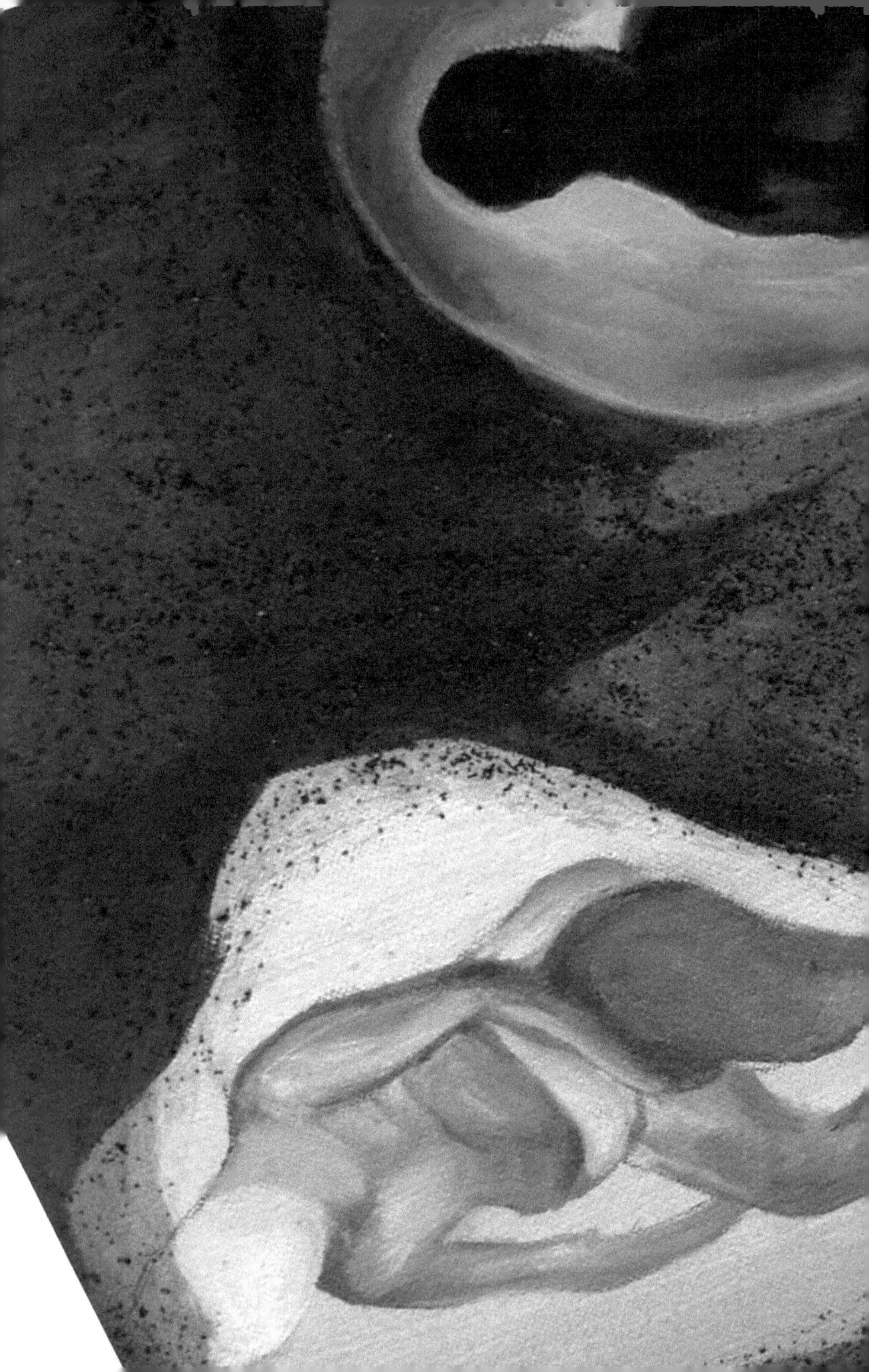

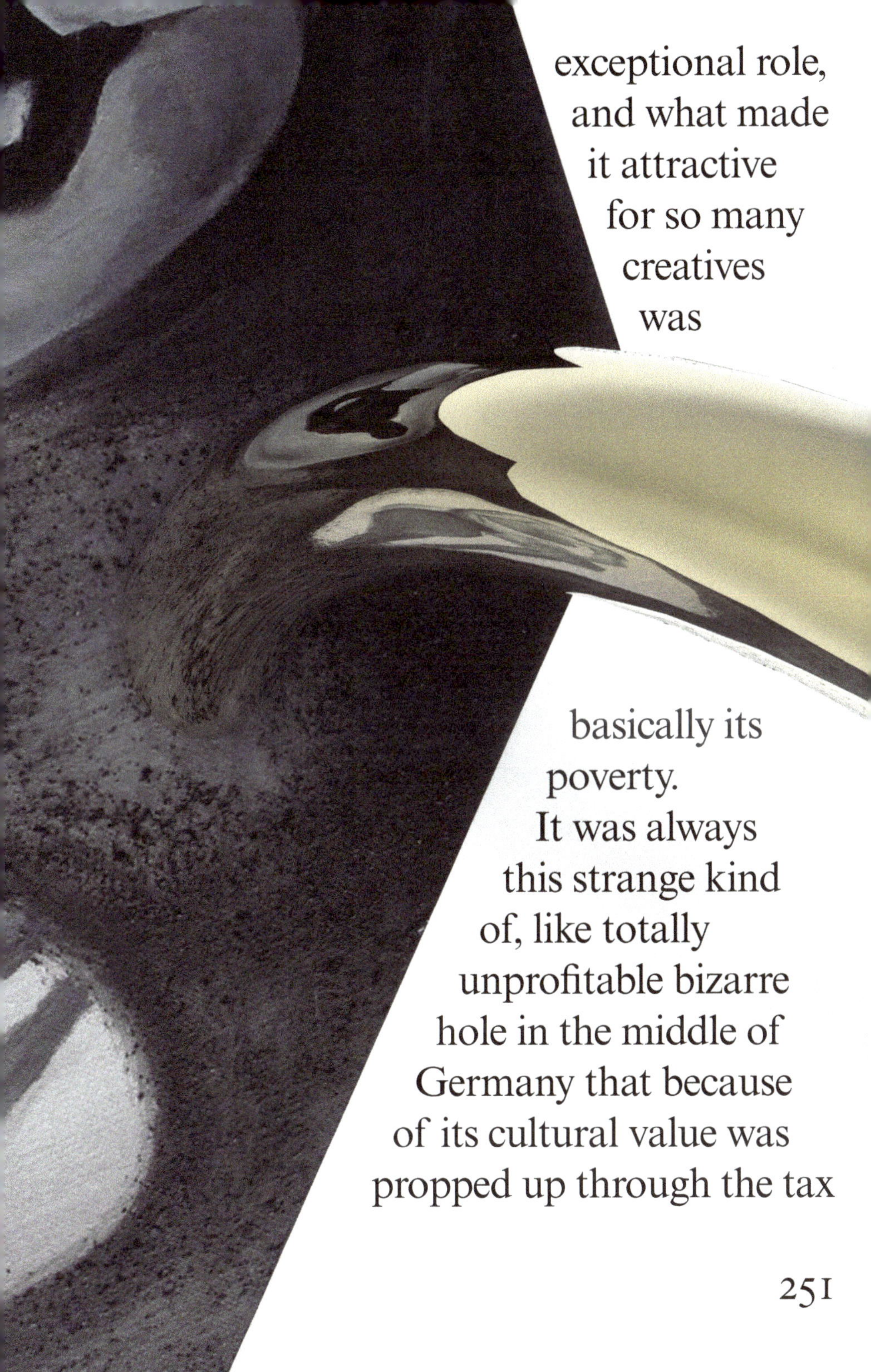

exceptional role,
and what made
it attractive
for so many
creatives
was

basically its
poverty.
It was always
this strange kind
of, like totally
unprofitable bizarre
hole in the middle of
Germany that because
of its cultural value was
propped up through the tax

money of the rest of Germany. Yeah I think it was definitely cooler other times. Even thinking about the 80s, the West Berlin in the 80s. Wow…

I think Berlin has always been the avant-garde epicenter even like during the Weimar Republic. I mean, after the wall fell, basically in the 90s, tons and tons of opportunists came in, and lots of artists who saw, oh there are so many empty spaces here for us to create stuff. And then, slowly more and more people have come in as Berlin has become more and more popular who kind of want to make a profit and are driving prices up.

But that's also a very simplistic way to look at it. I mean the wages are very very low. In all of Germany, wages have not risen in accordance with the prices of living rising. But in Berlin, it's been particularly extreme. Everything used to be so cheap here. And now things are coming to the same standard as the rest of Germany, but wages aren't rising. So yeah, that's really difficult. I mean everyone I know is living extremely precariously.

Is there no solution for this direction?

I think people need to organize themselves and put more pressure on the government to hear their needs and to meet them. I mean the city has so many secondary industries that are making so much cash off Berlin's reputation as an artistic city. But the money is just not reaching artists at all, it's reaching the hoteliers. It's reaching the restaurant owners. It's reaching the tourist guides. All of these different industries are profiting from cultural tourism. But the working class and artists are screwed.

And if the situation continues the way it is, the people who comprise the city's cultural capital are going to leave. And yeah, then the Berlin will be left with its youth hostels.

www.berlinartprize.com
www.zoemiller.eu

Zoë，柏林

2015年8月25日
采访于柏林Kreuzberg区

请自我介绍一下？

我叫Zoë Claire Miller。我在柏林生活了7年了。我是一名艺术家和活动组织者。我最近在做的一些比较大的项目包括：柏林艺术奖（Berlin Art Prize），这是一个由艺术家发起，艺术家运作的独立艺术奖项。另外还有时代大奖（Time Grants Campaign），那是一个呼吁为柏林的艺术设立更多公共基金奖项的活动。

你能介绍具体一下"柏林艺术奖"吗？

"柏林艺术奖"是由我和另外三位，艺术家，作家和艺术史学者一起在2013年创立的。我们产生创立这样一个奖项的想法是因为我们觉得柏林有那么多艺术家，艺术家人群超过一万以上，但是只有很少的艺术奖项真的在做些有意思的事，或是能向观众展示些激动人心的作品。

似乎很多奖项都是集团式的不知所云。比如垄断了柏林的能源和电力的Vattenfall集团，他们也有一个艺术奖项。但他们的奖项完全是关于他们的特权，而不是支持艺术。而所有的艺术机构和政府所设置的奖项又似乎总是颁给那些毫无悬念的候选人。只有当你已经在艺术市场非常成功的时候才能拿到那些奖项。

也有一些公共的艺术基金，但那些不是奖项。而且它们的数量非常少，媒体宣传也做得不够。你花了半个小时在市政府非常不用户友好的网站上，好不容易才能找到去年从柏林议院拿到奖助的那15位艺术家的名单。

我们也对品质形成和声誉建立的整个过程很感兴趣。大多数时候似乎都是一个从上而下的等级系统，那些已经有很多特权和金钱的人准备好了发表申明。“好的，我给你分享一点我的权力和特权，通过这样我让你的地位有所提升。”大多数时候的情况都是这样。

当你还很年轻的时候，如果你想要在艺术圈里成功，你需要找到一个有地位的人来把你当作他们的神童。但如果你的性格不符合达尔文的进化论竞争规律，或是你不知道怎么自我宣传，那就只能祝你好运了。

而我们想把这过程扭转过来，保留艺术奖项所有的标准流程和模式，但是以颠覆性的精神，从完全不同的角度出发。

所以柏林艺术奖包括一个有三十个左右提名艺术家的群展。所有被提名的艺术家的作品都会被展出。每年有三位艺术家得奖，他们会获得一些奖金。奖金的钱不多，因为我们并没有基金资助。所以基本上这笔奖金就是在我们付完其他所有开销之后剩下的。而大多数的经费我们都是在展览开幕当晚靠卖饮料筹集的。另外我们也会收到一些捐款。还有很多非常棒的当地赞助人给我们提供非常便宜价格的服务，比如免费打印，或是给我们提供材料。

奖金的钱主要是用来支付获奖艺术家去参加驻留项目的费用。这样他们就不用自己掏钱。每年的获奖艺术家都会获得在不同国家的驻留项目。第一年是在意大利，去年在乔治亚，今年是在希腊。

所以奖项本身并没有资金来源，基本上你们都得等到开幕那天晚上才能筹到？

是的，这并不是最理想的状况。我们总是忐忑不安，担心我们是不是能够筹到足够多的钱。去年我们不得不在开幕之后又搞了一次party来筹集资金缺口。非常遗憾的是柏林市并不愿意支持我们的奖项。虽然我觉得我们已经获得很多好评，并且为柏林和柏林的艺术家起了很多很好的媒体宣传作用。

哦，我忘了说奖项很重要的一个组成部分还包括一座奖杯。我们每年都请不同的艺术家来创作奖杯。对我们来说很重要的一点还在于，我们希望把大家聚集到一起，并尝试把每个人都放到同一个起跑线上。不用像其他那些奖项和竞赛一样强制要求每个艺术家根据某一特定主题创作，或是设定年龄限制，或是必须要有艺术学位。这些对我们来说都不重要。我们的奖项完全是不设任何限制的。只要你生活和工作在柏林，并且你已经在这呆了至少1年半以上，你就可以申请。其他的都不重要。

你们的网站上说奖项的颁发完全是基于作品的艺术水准。但是艺术水准的标准到底是什么呢？因为当你和一些人一起挑选作品和艺术家的时候，不可避免的总是会存在主观偏好。所以你们的挑选过程是怎样的？

当然这总是非常非常主观的。到底艺术水准是什么我觉得也很难用语言来形容。但是基本上评选的结果就是每个参与奖项筹备工作人员和评委会成员对于他们所认为的艺术水准标准的总和。

每年我们都有不同的评委。我们邀请评委过目所有申请人的作品。我们的工作人员也会浏览所有申请，然后我们再决定哪些人获得提名。最后评委们挑选出谁是最终的获奖者。你会发现有时候评委的观点非常不同，但有时候又惊人的相似。今年评委们说，“哦，我们看到作品后10分钟之内就决定了谁会获奖。”

每年有多少人申请？

基本上平均每年的申请人数都在1000人左右。

组织这个奖项会占用你多少时间？

这很难说，因为很多时间都和其他工作时间交织在一起了。像是回邮件，打电话这种，很多都和我回复其他邮件和电话的时间是交叉的。但是在展览开始之前和展览进行中需要全职投入的时间绝对有三个月。

那你是怎么给自己付工资的呢？

没有人拿任何报酬。

3到4个月的全职工作却没有任何报酬？

是的。我也不知道我们是怎么办到的。这非常疯狂。我是说，整个柏林艺术奖的过程就像是一个完全不可理喻的疯狂想法不知怎么居然实现了。而这里面有很多部分看上去都是非常让人费解的。就好像，这是怎么可能做到的？不过我们也知道这是很难持续的。因为对于我和其他几个在最主要投入精力的人来说，这是一件从情感和体力上都很消耗的事。我们每次在颁奖开幕展览结束之后都会觉得完全透支。我会觉得被耗尽了。是的，我们需要找到其他解决办法。

听上去，你和其他一些艺术家想要做些对艺术家社群有益的事，但是你们却首先无法获得自我支撑？

对，我们每个人都非常没有安全感。我觉得这是一个特别极端的例子。柏林艺术奖对外给人的印象很专业，因为我们有非常好的专业平面设计师帮我们设计网站和形象。所以很多没有做过调查的人会以为我们很有钱。好像会有神奇的资金从不知道哪里冒出来一样。这挺好玩的，但是也挺悲剧的。

你们有考虑过以后可能会怎么办吗？

是的。目前为止，我们还没有拿到过任何公共性艺术基金的支持。但是我觉得我们必须要拿到公共基金才可能继续。要么我们就找到一个非常大的赞助商愿意真的来投资我们。因为到目前为止，我们总是说，“哦，我们不想要和大品牌的名字有什么关联。”但这很可能是能让这个奖项继续下去的唯一可能性。

其实这也挺冒险的，当品牌给你赞助的时候，一方面来说，那对他们是宣传和品牌包装的方式；另一方面，他们是不是愿意真的给你自由，会不会想要参与进来指手划脚？

对，这是一个问题。这也是为什么我们目前为止总是想要和更多数量而且多元化的赞助商合作的原因。他们当然都有各自的诉求和他们想要从柏林艺术奖中获得的东西。但是至少绝对没有人干涉我们要做什么。这是非常明确的。当然，也是因为几乎没有人给我们现金资助。所以他们怎么可能期望告诉我们什么该做什么不该做呢。

所以他们只是给你们提供免费的服务？

是的。

你之前提到有一千名艺术家申请，但只有三个人能拿到奖项。你觉得那些被拒绝的人应该如何面对这一状况呢？

我觉得竞争这么激烈更应被看作是一种安慰。如果我们有钱的话，如果可能，每年我都觉得有上百人应该得到提名。但是我们不得不把名额缩小。我觉得这是非常主观的选择，没人应该因为被拒绝而感到沮丧。当然这说起来容易做到却很难。

不过，我也的确发现有非常多的艺术家作品做得很棒，但是在准备作品集和介绍自己的作品时却并不在行。还有很多艺术家选择什么介绍都不写。因为我们说作品介绍是可选项。但是很显然，有些类型的作品并不是那么一目了然。所以如果能给出理解作品的上下文语境会很有帮助。

作为艺术奖项的一部分，我们每年都会给艺

术家提供免费的公开课，教授大家例如："理想的作品集是什么样的？""怎样才能让观众更好地理解你的作品？""如何提供足够的信息，不多也不少。"而且我觉得艺术家应该更经常地寻求帮助。每个人都会有平面设计师的朋友，每个人都有可以写艺术类文章的学艺术史的朋友。所以艺术家们应该多请他们帮忙。

不过当然，你总会看到作品的图片和实际作品之间的差异。这也是为什么我们要求在评委决定谁最终获得大奖之前，被提名的艺术家需要提交真实的作品，并来现场布展。所以并不是全都凭借PDF来判断。

你之前提到说柏林有一万多名艺术家，这个数字是从哪里来的？

在德国，有一种特别为艺术家提供的退休金/社会保险叫做KSK。所以当然保险发放机构会知道艺术家的数量。或者说他们知道那些已经被他们接受的艺术家的数量。但是要获得这个保险有一些先决条件，如果你还不能通过你的艺术来赚到足够多的钱，那你也没法买这种保险。但如果你的其他工作赚到的钱超过一定数额，那你也没法买这种保险。但只要你进入了这个保险系统，那它基本上就可以补贴你健康保险的费用。

也就是说那一万名艺术家是已经能靠卖作品生活的？

是的。但是通常那些已经非常成功的艺术家是不会继续买这种保险，因为他们会需要付更多的保险金。这个保险系统是根据你的收入来决定保费的。所以如果你赚很多钱，那你也就要付更多的保费。同时，还有很多艺术家根本都还进不了这个保险系统，因为他们的作品不够商业。

所以柏林实际艺术家的数量可能要更多？

绝对的。因为我们还要考虑到那些只是在柏林呆上一阵子的艺术家，他们并没有进入这个德国艺术家保险的系统。或者还有一些人在欧洲或世界的其他什么地方拥有他们的保险。有很多艺术家现在在柏林，但是他们只打算在这呆上一两年的时间。

现在柏林的艺术圈正在发生什么？

我觉得之前最流行的绝对是"后网络艺术"，但现在那好像已经变成了一个贬义词。过去被认为是"后网络艺术家"的一些人都不愿意被称之为"后网络"了。很多艺术家在创作和科技，品牌美学，反乌托邦，未来主义愿景，后人类等和眼下正流行的"加速主义"理论相关的作品。

除此以外，我觉得还有一些带有非常强烈地域特征的艺术，是只有你看过了其他地方的艺术并有所比较后才能意识到你所在地方的艺术有什么不一样的。

你能举个例子吗？

当你看美国的艺术的时候，或者就说在纽约吧，因为那是美国最重要的艺术重地。你会看到很多有关波普艺术，流行文化的作品。但那样的作品在德国就不成立。这里的人会觉得那太肤浅了。波普艺术似乎是人们提起美国艺术史时最常回顾的。而在这里我觉得可能现代主义的其他分支会更受重视。柏林的艺术最典型的有一阵子就是那种非常男性化的，摇滚，黑暗坏男孩类型的作品。你可以去看一下Guido Baudach画廊代理的艺术家的作品。我觉得这种风格可能跟这里漫长又寒冷的冬天有关吧。

柏林给我的印象非常完美，简直是艺术和艺术家的天堂。真的是这样吗？你有看到什么问题吗？

当然有很多问题。不管在哪里都会存在问题。但是目前我们在这里所面临的最大问题绝对是生活成本的不断提高。艺术家们越来越难找到可以负担地起的工作室。情况对于居住在这里的艺术家来说正在变得越来越糟。当然，这是在哪里都存在的问题，这就是资本主义和不负责任的政府太晚意识到问题，或者要么根本就不在乎。

柏林在很长时间都保有其非常独特的角色，而它之所以对创意人士充满吸引力的原因恰恰就在于它的贫穷。柏林一直都好像在德国中间的一个完全无法盈利的怪洞。而它的文化价值都是依靠德国其他地方的税款来支撑的。就算只是回想一下80年代的西柏林，喔！

我觉得柏林一直都是非常前卫的文化中心，即使是在魏玛共和国时期。90年代柏林墙被推翻之后，许多机会主义者涌入了柏林。很多艺术家也突然发现柏林有那么多空置的空间可以用来创作。但是慢慢地随着柏林越来越受欢迎，很多人来到这里想要从中谋利。并导致了价格的上涨。

这当然是非常简单化的看法。但是，这里的工资水平真的非常非常低。在整个德国，工资水平都没有相应地随着生活成本的提高而提升，在柏林尤为极端。过去这里的东西都很便宜，现在却和德国其他地方的物价差不多了，而薪水却一直没有增长。所以真的很困难。每个人都在充满危机感地生活。

难道这个问题没有任何解决方法吗？

我觉得人们需要组织起来，并给政府施加更多压力。让政府听到民众的需求并满足他们。这个城市有那么多第二产业在依靠柏林作为艺术都市的声誉赚钱。但是这些钱却根本不会让艺术家得到什么好处。旅馆，餐厅，导游，所有这些行业都在靠文化旅游获利。但是工薪阶级和艺术家们所面临的情况却在越变越糟。

如果再这样发展下去，那些构成了柏林文化资本的人就不得不离开。那时候柏林就会只剩下青年旅馆了。

www.berlinartprize.com
www.zoemiller.eu

Paintings on page. 32/33, 50/51, 60/61, 70/71, 80/81, 110/111, 118/119, 136/137, 170/171, 188/189, 228/229, 230/231, 240/241, 250/251 by **Wang Zi Yun,**
Born in 1986, Nanjing. Lives and works in Hangzhou. She is currently a doctoral candidate in Painting Practice and Theory at China Academy of Art.

'The figures in my paintings have almost all been with me quietly for a long time. They intrigue me in one way or another. Sometimes it's their faces, sometimes it's the posture, their original identity, or their surroundings. I find them fantastic and mysterious.

Although I don't really care about these aspects when I paint. They have lost their original meanings. Rather, they are revealing as physical appearances, as if they are some random pressed paper that can be thrown into the trashcan the next second.

I like that my models are fragile and distant. I'm also interested in their otherness.

Or, in other words, our gaze into each other. What I'm doing is a bit like one-sided registration, declaring temporary ownership somehow.

During my painting process I embrace chance, while carefully avoiding repetition and too much straightforwardness. Often times, what comes out is far from what I initially went for. But that's also when interesting things come out from the paintings by themselves. There is surprise every time. And that's the part I like about it.'

www.zyunzyun.com

本册 32/33，50/51，60/61，70/71，80/81，110/111，118/119，136/137，170/171，188/189，228/229，230/231，240/241，250/251页中油画作者为王子芸，

1986年出生于南京，生活工作于杭州。中国美院绘画实践与理论博士在读。

“我的模特儿们几乎都默默和我相处了很长时间，可能它们在某方面吸引我，比如某张面孔某个姿态，或者它们原本的身份，所在的环境，产生些奇妙的感觉。但其实这些信息我也是不关心的。它们已经没有原来的意义，更多呈现的是物性，像是一摞随处可见的压扁的纸片儿，可能下一秒就丢进垃圾筒。我喜欢它们的脆弱，冷冰冰。同时也感兴趣这些“他人”，或者说是自己和他人间的互相凝视。我所做的，有点像是一厢情愿地非要给它们注册，算是一种短暂的占有吧。然而画画的过程我很随机，也很谨慎，尽量避免重复和直白。经常折腾得已经和初衷相差太远，就会有些奇妙的东西自己从画里跑出来了，每次惊喜都不重样，这是我比较喜欢的部分。”

www.zyunzyun.com

[soft] magazine
Creative People and Their Day Jobs
June 2016, Issue 2

Interview: Chen Zou
Translation: Chen Zou
Proofreading: Alex Kopecky
Design: Weiyi Li

Open Art is an online media platform introducing quality art related content and information to the Chinese artist community. For further information, contact hello@open-art.co or visit www.open-art.co

[soft]
全球年轻艺术家访谈杂志
2016年6月　第2期

采访：邹晨
翻译：邹晨
英文校对：Alex Kopecky
设计：李维伊

www.open-art.co

www.ingramcontent.com/pod-product-compliance
Ingram Content Group UK Ltd.
Pitfield, Milton Keynes, MK11 3LW, UK
UKHW062306290726
14090UKWH00018B/915